Dear Duncan,

Thank you for all the help and fun times over the years. Although you will know most of the things in here, I hope you like the quotes at chapter start.

All my best,

A Guide to Starting Your Hedge Fund

**Erik Serrano Berntsen
and John Thompson**

WILEY

To Ada and Mary Grace

Contents

Acknowledgements

We would like to thank all the colleagues and co-investors who we have had the pleasure of working with over the years. Many of them will hopefully recognize themselves in some of the more amusing stories contained herein. We would also like to thank David Lee who has been invaluable in getting the text over the finishing line and has helped with fact checking, data gathering, legal background work, moral support, and great quotes. We appreciate the input of all those who contributed comments on manuscript drafts, including Dieter Kaiser and Markus Kreutzer for the detailed proof reviews.

The Wiley publishing team has been a wonderful group of professionals to work with since our first meeting in Chichester all those years ago. We thank the ones that are no longer there, and all the ones who helped us in the last year to bring the project to fruition, including Thomas Hyrkiel, Jennie Kitchin, Sam Hartley, and the design team for its most fantastic cover artwork (not only is launching your fund a maze but it's a hedge-maze, genius).

Thank you to the Stable Asset Management team who make every long work day a pleasure, and to all the managers we have backed and seeded over the years who keep surprising us with their tenacity and results. We are very proud of being associated with such talented and fundamentally solid human beings.

Many thanks to all the lawyers, administrators, auditors, accountants, marketers, and directors with whom we have debated the issues contained in the book. This has been almost as much fun as working with you on our investments. To all those who waited for a few years since their first pre-order to final delivery, thank you for not cancelling the orders. We hope to confirm that good things come to those who wait.

PART I

WHY THIS BOOK?

Chapter 1

Introduction

Beginning is half the journey.
Traditional Korean proverb

Why This Book?

When we launched our first hedge fund in 2006 we needed guidance. As a firm we had over three decades of experience in all facets of the energy industry as well as a background in management consulting and private equity. This rooted our approach in developing detailed business strategies and understanding the best practices for both young and mature businesses. What we did not have was an understanding of what it took to start and manage a hedge fund, especially a hedge fund focused on investing in energy and related commodities markets. As we looked for resources to help us fill our knowledge gap, we realized there was nothing out there.

Since those early days we have partnered with some of the best commodity traders and commodity investors to launch institutional quality asset managers. It has been a fascinating journey filled with a rollercoaster of events as varied as the 2008 Global Financial Crisis (GFC), the Bernard Madoff scandal, a day when we thought our investment bank clearers would go under, the end of Swiss banking secrecy, a deluge of new regulations, the exit of most banks from commodity trading, and a bunch of fantastic colleagues. We have also been blessed with great investors who we feel privileged to serve. Of course, along the way we have learned many lessons. Though some of these lessons came from success (or perhaps more accurately, serendipity), the majority of the lessons we have learned were the result of mistakes we made along the way.

As we reflected back on those days of perusing bookshelves for books to help us with launching our first hedge fund, we thought it might be worthwhile to distil some of the lessons that we had learned over the years and record them. We wanted to create the book that we wished we had when we started down this path.

It was a great idea. Unfortunately, like many projects of any worth, it took much longer than we had anticipated. Thankfully, after many years, we are grateful that we can finally present this book to you.

We do not pretend that this book is exhaustive. That said, we feel it will be a useful reference tool for hedge fund practitioners. Specifically both energy commodity hedge fund managers as well as investors in such hedge funds should find it particularly useful. At least that is our hope.

The Big Picture and Energy Commodities

The amount of capital invested in hedge funds is approaching USD 3 trillion. To put that in context, the amount of capital invested in hedge funds is greater than the individual nominal 2012 GDP of France (USD 2.6 trillion), the UK (USD 2.5 trillion), and Russia (USD 2 trillion). Even the combined nominal 2012 GDP of countries like Australia (USD 1.5 trillion) and South Korea (USD 1.1. trillion) does not equal the amount of capital invested in hedge funds. In fact, the USA, China, Japan, and Germany are the only countries that on an individual basis have a nominal 2012 GDP that surpasses the amount of capital invested in hedge funds. It is anticipated that more capital will flow to hedge funds, with total hedge fund assets under management to nearly double and hit USD 6 trillion by 2018.[1]

Undoubtedly, it is an interesting time to be involved in the alternative investments industry. From the end of World War II until the present day, we have seen the growth and institutionalization of corporate and national pensions, endowments, foundations, family offices, and other similar entities responsible for directing much of the approximately USD 3 trillion that is invested in hedge funds.

With the spectre of underfunded pension liabilities looming over many developed economies, alternative investments have emerged as a preferred asset class to help generate attractive, risk-adjusted returns that ideally have minimal correlation to traditional asset classes. Indeed, for many large pensions and other large pools of capital that are under liabilities pressure, 'alternative investments' have become an increasingly important part of portfolio construction.

---

[1]Citi Investor Services, *Opportunities and Challenges for Hedge Funds in the Coming Era of Optimization, Part 1: Changes Driven by the Investor Audience*, 2014.

Within this milieu, many investors in alternatives are looking to commodities and especially energy commodities to provide attractive, uncorrelated – if sometimes volatile – returns that form one component of a larger, diversified portfolio that likely includes both traditional and alternative investments. Oil has long been traded by hedge funds and other speculative capital pools. Electricity, the fuels for generating electricity, and so-called environmental products such as emissions credits and weather derivatives have become high-profile investment strategies offering the promise of potentially high uncorrelated returns.

These high returns, however, are accompanied by volatility and risk. Additionally, few investors have experience in evaluating these investment opportunities and few prospective hedge fund managers understand the market fundamentals and their associated risks. Many financial institutions and service providers have only begun to dedicate financial and intellectual capital to these rapidly growing investment strategies.

Case Study: Amaranth Advisors

For better or worse, the hedge fund that has become virtually synonymous with the volatility and risk related to energy commodities investing is Amaranth Advisors ('Amaranth'). Amaranth's spectacular demise in 2006, however, belied its more modest beginnings as a multi-strategy hedge fund launched in Greenwich, CT, in 2000 that was focused on convertible arbitrage opportunities. As convertible arbitrage opportunities and related profits began declining, Amaranth transitioned to an investment strategy that focused on energy commodities. Eventually, energy investing accounted for approximately 80% of Amaranth's profits, with its main fund growing to over USD 9 billion dollars by August 2006. Unfortunately, that would be the peak of Amaranth's success.

In 2004, about two years before its implosion, Amaranth hired a natural gas trader named Brian Hunter. Hunter had worked as a natural gas futures trader for both a pipeline company and then for Deutsche Bank before joining Amaranth. In 2005, Hunter was so instrumental in helping generate USD 1 billion of profits for Amaranth that it was expected his bonus might be as high as USD 100 million. Hunter's natural gas trading strategy focused on spread trades using natural gas futures. In this strategy, traders enter into long and short positions in the same underlying and benefit from the difference in pricing over time, or the *spread*. In addition to natural gas futures, Hunter overlaid call and put options on the underlying natural gas future contracts as well as natural gas swap contracts that enhanced his core spread trade strategy using natural gas futures.

In early 2006, Hunter continued his spread trading strategy by buying natural gas futures contracts, options, and swaps for winter delivery, shorting non-winter-month gas futures, and entering similar positions via options and swaps. The maturity of these contracts ranged from 2006 until 2010. This strategy served Hunter and Amaranth well through the spring of 2006, when Amaranth's energy investments were up approximately USD 2 billion by April. In May, the long-dated natural gas future positions entered a period of volatility, although trouble was not immediately apparent.

After peaking at over USD 9 billion in August, Amaranth's main fund experienced a significant drawdown in September 2006 as the natural gas positions Hunter had taken started moving against him. By the middle of September, the fund had experienced a 50% drawdown and had a single day loss in September of USD 560 million. As the fund had difficulties meeting the ever-increasing size of margin calls, eventually market participants purchased large stakes of Amaranth's natural gas positions. The natural gas markets eventually stabilized towards the end of September 2006. Unfortunately, Amaranth's loss led to the closing of its doors and Amaranth and Hunter have been involved in a variety of regulatory investigations and legal actions since then. Amaranth, named after a flower meaning 'unfading' or 'eternal' in Greek, appears as though it will live up to its namesake, albeit for the wrong reasons.

Layout

With the hope of helping you launch a fund or invest in an energy commodities hedge fund that becomes an institutional quality asset manager and not another Amaranth, we have organized this book in a way that we think will allow it to be used as a reference guide as different issues or topics arise. Beyond this Introduction, comprising Part I, the book has four further parts and a series of appendices.

Part II provides the basics and background of hedge funds, energy commodities, and trading energy commodities. Part III delves into the key areas of starting a hedge fund with the focus on a sound business plan, the legal requirements of starting a hedge fund, and working with service providers such as prime brokers and administrators. Part IV focuses on the nuts and bolts of running an investment management firm by exploring topics of fundraising and operations. Part V concludes with points that hedge fund investors should consider when adding an energy commodity hedge fund to their portfolio, as well as thoughts we have had on the future of energy commodity hedge funds. The appendices include outlines of a sample business plan, an offering memorandum (also referred to as a private placement memorandum or PPM), and a due diligence questionnaire.

The Beginning

We have come a long way since trying to figure out how to launch our first energy commodities hedge fund almost a decade ago. Like us, the alternative investments industry, and hedge funds in particular, have come a long way in the last few years. We hope the beginning of this journey for you ends up being as rewarding as it has been for us. It is an incredible time to be part of an exciting and dynamic industry. Although the hedge fund industry has matured considerably since Alfred Winslow Jones started the first hedge fund in 1949, perhaps a review of the past is the best place to begin your journey.

Bibliography

Chincarini, L. (2008) A case study on risk management: Lessons from the collapse of Amaranth Advisors L.L.C. *Journal of Applied Finance* 18(1). Available at: ssrn.com/abstract=1304859.

Citi Investor Services (2014) *Opportunities and Challenges for Hedge Funds in the Coming Era of Optimization, Part 1: Changes Driven by the Investor Audience.*

Till, H. (2007) The Amaranth Collapse: What happened and what have we learned thus far? EDHEC Case Study, August.

PART II
THE BASICS

Chapter 2

What Is a Hedge Fund?

Ever wonder why fund managers can't beat the S&P 500? Cause they're
sheep and the sheep get slaughtered.
Michael Douglas as Gordon Gecko, *Wall Street*

I Already Know What a Hedge Fund Is

If you are reading this book, you are likely already familiar with hedge funds. Accordingly, you might wonder why this chapter was included. At one level, this chapter was written for those new to the hedge fund universe who may find themselves reading this book. For these readers, this chapter can serve as an informative standalone section, or as a foundation for the more technical topics that will be covered later.

We think this chapter is also important for readers with more experience in dealing with hedge funds. Although the factual information itself may not be new to you, we try to present the information in a way that conveys the importance of perspective, which is a theme throughout this book.

Depending on your perspective, a hedge fund can represent different things. For the trader that recently started a hedge fund, it is more than just a technical definition. It represents a new business venture where very likely a large portion of a hedge fund founder's personal wealth and all of their personal reputation is invested. For the university endowment or asset manager who has placed money with a hedge fund, it can represent an investment in an asset class. To a lawmaker or regulator, a hedge fund is a nebulous, sometimes polemical component of the financial ecosystem. Of course, the general public's perception of hedge funds probably lies somewhere between a complete unawareness of them or and believing that hedge funds are populated by the likes of Gordon Gecko, the 'greed is good' character featured in the movie *Wall Street*.

A Little Bit of History

To the average person, hedge funds occupy the rarefied air of high finance populated by brash 'masters of the universe' whiz kids and erstwhile rocket scientists more interested in plying their numeric genius chasing dollars than conquering space. The glamour associated with hedge funds belies their more humble roots.

In 1949, at the age of 48, Alfred Winslow Jones launched what would become known as the first hedge fund by raising $60,000 to supplement the $40,000 he personally invested. With the princely sum of $100,000, Jones launched his investment firm, eponymously named A.W. Jones & Co. In terms of 2012 dollars, A.W. Jones & Co. was launched with slightly less than $1 million. Six decades later, A.W. Jones & Co. still exists, having evolved into a fund of hedge funds, now managing close to $300 million.

In terms of age, background, and interests, Jones does not fit the image that most have when thinking of the modern-day hedge fund manager. He started in finance at a late age and his background does not suggest any extraordinary quantitative aptitude. Indeed, for much of his life it seems that Jones was not motivated by making money, but was more focused on trying to understand the world and make it a bit better.

Jones was born to American parents in Melbourne, Australia. His family returned to the USA when he was four. After graduating from Harvard in 1923, Jones worked on a tramp steamer sailing all over the world before becoming a diplomat with the US Department of State. He eventually left the State Department and returned to school, receiving a PhD in sociology from Columbia in 1941. An article based on his PhD dissertation examining the zeitgeist of 1930s industrial workers in Akron, OH, was published in *Fortune*, eventually leading to a job there.

For most of the 1940s, Jones was a journalist at *Fortune* where he wrote on a wide variety of topics that largely had nothing to do with finance. In the first nearly 50 years of his life, the father of the hedge fund industry had been a student, sailor, diplomat, and journalist. Until this point, nothing in Jones' life indicated any special interest in the world of finance. This would change in 1949.

In early 1949, Jones wrote an article for *Fortune* entitled 'Fashions in Forecasting', where he profiled a number of investors and their respective investment methodologies. The process of researching and writing the article (available on the A.W. Jones & Co. website) seemingly inspired Jones, and with the aforementioned $100,000 he formed A.W. Jones & Co., an investment partnership that returned 17.3% in its first year. Not bad for a near 50-year-old journalist with a PhD in sociology.

But Jones' journey did not stop there. During the latter part of his life Jones worked with the Peace Corps, and at one point attempted to start a programme where young people from developing countries would come to the USA and serve as a cadre of Peace Corp-type volunteers working in the neediest areas of the country. The ethos of the curious, idealistic student who walked from Harvard Yard on to a freighter seemingly never faded, even after his years as an investor on Wall Street.

So What Is a Hedge Fund?

In her 1966 *Fortune* article 'The Jones Nobody Keeps Up With', Carol Loomis, a near-legendary figure at *Fortune*, wrote a profile on Jones and his firm. Her article describes Jones' path from sociology to Wall Street and the unique characteristics of his firm that have come to shape modern-day hedge funds. Indeed, it was Loomis' article that initially coined the phrase 'hedge fund'.

The management and investment practices employed by Jones served as the original template for other hedge funds that followed. Though today's hedge funds may only subscribe to the following in varying degrees, the below factors are still worth noting.

1. **Organizational structure.** A.W. Jones & Co. was formed as a partnership composed of general partners (GPs) and limited partners (LPs). Most hedge funds are constructed the same way today. GPs serve as managers of the fund and are responsible for investing its capital. Additionally, like Jones, GPs often invest a substantial amount of their own personal wealth in their funds. Depending on jurisdiction, GPs can be personally and severally liable for any debts or expenses incurred by the fund.

   In contrast, LPs act solely as investors in the fund and generally do not have any direct responsibility for the management of the fund or decision-making responsibility regarding how the fund deploys its capital. Unlike GPs, LP liability only extends to the amount of their investment in the fund.

2. **Fees.** Besides the use of a partnership structure for his firm, Jones introduced a performance-based incentive fee of 20%. This practice of receiving a performance fee has become ubiquitous among hedge funds, evolving to be embodied in the phrase '2 and 20'. The '2' refers to the management fee (2% of all invested capital that the fund manager uses

to cover administrative and operational costs such as office space, computers, and salary); '20' indicates the performance fee (20% of all profits that the fund generates). Sometimes the performance fee is taken only after a specified hurdle rate has been achieved and frequently only when a high-water mark has been surpassed.

Although '2 and 20' is standard in the hedge fund industry, fee structure has become an important point of negotiation when investors place their capital with a fund. Different management and performance fees can be negotiated. For example, a fund may take a smaller management fee in return for a performance fee higher than 20%, or if an investor is willing to agree to a longer lock-up period for their capital. That said, '2 and 20' is considered an industry standard fee structure from which to commence bargaining, if any.

3. **Leverage.** Jones employed leverage to purchase a greater number of shares for companies he was optimistic about. Though using leverage was not completely unique at the time, using leverage to magnify returns was not a common practice among long-only mutual funds. Depending on investment strategy, leverage is still commonly used by hedge funds today.

4. **Short selling.** Jones used short selling to decrease the risk implicit in his portfolio. By selling shares, Jones helped manage his portfolio against the vagaries of the market, that the performance of his portfolio was driven by the stocks he had picked. This allowed him to protect, or 'hedge', his portfolio. Jones focused his hedging efforts on reducing market exposure with the aim of making the performance of his fund more correlated to his selection of equities, and less a function of overall market performance.

The short selling practiced by Jones underlies what is commonly referred to as a long/short strategy, which describes the approach of many hedge funds today. There are funds, however, that choose not to hedge their positions at all, either through short selling or otherwise, and no longer follow Jones' footsteps on this point. Additionally, some funds use short selling to take risk as opposed to mitigating risk. For example, short selling is used by funds to profit when they feel a company will decline in value.

Jones coined his newfound concept as a 'hedged fund' all those years ago denoting some protection from the overall market. Today, some hedge funds are not actually hedged, although many of their investors may think they are and so they benefit from the original nomenclature.

As noted previously, modern-day hedge funds may differ on some of the points listed above, although these four factors originally found in A.W. Jones & Co. served as the archetype for hedge funds as the industry evolved post-1949. Additionally, many hedge funds share the following three characteristics that have emerged as hedge funds have matured.

1. **Hedge funds are considered alternative investments.** Compared with traditional investments such as equities or bonds, hedge fund investments belong to the universe of so-called 'alternative' investments. This world is also home to private equity and venture capital investments. The main features of alternative investments include:

   o   they are not traded on a public market, which decreases their liquidity and increases their valuation complexity;
   o   they have inflexible redemption policies with longer lock-ups;
   o   the use of leverage to magnify returns often plays an important role in their strategy;
   o   there are regulatory restrictions around their eligible investor base and the nature of their advertising;[2] and
   o   there is still generally little regulation around fee levels and structures, which tend to be performance rather than asset-based.

2. **Hedge funds are focused on absolute returns.** As we saw in our review of the origin of hedge funds, one of the original objectives of their distinct investment strategy was to decrease exposure to the general market. A major selling point of hedge funds is their promise of absolute returns – positive returns independent of market performance.

   This objective – and promise – is in stark contrast to the relative return objectives of traditional investments. A relative return measures how well an investment has performed against a benchmark, and the investment is deemed to have met its goal if it has performed better relative to that benchmark. For example, if a fund aims to deliver higher relative returns than the stock market, fund performance of –5% in a year when the stock market drops 10% is deemed successful by only having lost 5% of its value relative to its benchmark. Many would argue that relative return objectives are not particularly compelling. As a well-known industry saying goes, you can't eat relative returns.

---

[2]Note that the Jumpstart Our Business Startups Act ("JOBS Act"), which was passed into law by the United States in 2012, removed restrictions on general solicitation though accredited investor requirements generally still apply.

It is worthwhile to point out that although hedge funds are focused on absolute returns, hedge funds are frequently included in investor portfolios for diversification purposes. In particular, energy commodity hedge funds can serve a diversifying role in a balanced portfolio.

3. **Hedge funds value information.** Hedge funds are typically very secretive about their operations. The financial press has sometimes interpreted this behaviour as Machiavellian. This is not entirely justified, however, as it is reasonable that hedge funds are reluctant to share information about their investors, size of assets under management, and trading and investment strategies. It is logical to protect one's edge, bearing in mind that diffusion of proprietary information could erode it.

Hedge Funds (Un)Defined

Thus far, we have listed some important characteristics that describe aspects of many hedge funds. We realize, however, that a definition has not been offered. This is because a universally accepted definition of a hedge fund does not exist. Indeed, if one were to ask a group of hedge fund managers to define what a hedge fund is, a series of similar, partially overlapping answers would emerge, but it would be unlikely any were exactly the same.

This is partly because there are various types of hedge funds that use different types of investment strategies. These experiences shape how these individual fund managers define the term 'hedge fund'. Perhaps more importantly, however, is that hedge funds remain relatively unregulated and, as such, a formal, legal definition has not emerged. Although there are restrictions on the number of investors and the types of investors that invest in hedge funds, these rules were not crafted to apply only to hedge funds. Chapter 6 contains an in-depth discussion on the legal aspects of hedge fund formation and management.

Indeed, the very term 'hedge fund' may actually be a misnomer. The hedging nature of the original hedge funds was a defining characteristic for naming purposes, but probably not appropriate from a descriptive point of view. Jones' contemporary 'hedge funds' were not focused on hedging risk; they were more focused on employing leverage.

Although a legal definition does not yet exist, government agencies and regulators have tried to describe hedge funds. In 2003, the US Securities and Exchange Commission's (SEC's) Staff Report on hedge funds defined a hedge fund as '...an entity that holds a pool of securities and perhaps other assets, whose interests are not sold in a registered public offering and which is not registered as an investment company under the Investment Company Act'.[3]

Those who detect the distinctly nebulous tone of the SEC will not be surprised to find that the definition has not advanced much since the SEC's 35th Annual Report in 1969. The imprecise nature of the SEC definition is part of what hedge funds are, namely investment vehicles lacking concrete classification. The SEC definition does, however, capture some of the key defining features of hedge funds. There are a number of high-level features, many of which were highlighted earlier, that most hedge funds share, and it is through these shared qualities that one can most accurately and practically define what a hedge fund is.

Unfortunately, to date, securities laws do not have an exact definition of the term 'hedge fund'. Admittedly, there has been increased regulatory focus on hedge funds following the 2008 GFC. For example, in response to the crisis, the US government passed the Dodd–Frank Wall Street Reform and Consumer Protection Act ('Dodd–Frank').

Title IV of Dodd–Frank is called 'Regulation Of Advisers To Hedge Funds And Others'. Unhelpfully, the term 'hedge funds' is only mentioned in the title but never mentioned again in the body of Title IV. This section, *inter alia*, imposes a registration requirement for hedge funds that meet certain criteria. This registration requirement did not exist before, which contributed to the perception that hedge funds operated in secrecy. For better or worse, hedge funds continue to fall under the generic definition of 'private fund' found in the Investment Advisers Act of 1940, the same Act that Jones referenced when he started his firm.

So, returning to the SEC's 2003 Staff Report on hedge funds, the report offered the following hedge fund definition. A hedge fund is:

> ...an entity that holds a pool of securities and perhaps other assets, whose interests are not sold in a registered public offering and which is not registered as an investment company under the Investment Company Act...
>
> Hedge fund strategies may include short selling, arbitrage, hedging, leverage, concentration, investing in distressed or bankrupt companies, investing in derivatives, investing in privately issued securities, or investing in volatile international markets.

---

[3]For perhaps a clearer definition of what a hedge fund is, please refer to the International Organization of Secutities Commissions' consultation report titled *Hedge Funds Oversight* (March 2009) available at www.iosco.org.

Perhaps the broad definition offered by the SEC is apropos given the diversity of hedge funds employing varied strategies that exist today. Jones likely could not have imagined that his 1949 article on different investment methods would have such a profound impact on his life as well as the world of finance.

The Growth of the Hedge Fund Industry

The most visible evidence of Jones' impact is the tremendous growth the hedge fund industry has seen over the last few decades, and in particular the last 10 to 15 years. As mentioned in the Introduction, it is estimated that hedge funds manage approximately $3 trillion.[4] Undoubtedly, the number of hedge funds and the assets they manage have grown considerably. This upward trend indicates that hedge funds are no longer solely the purview of family offices and high-net-worth individuals sitting in a Park Avenue penthouse. Much of the recent growth of the industry can be attributed to a few drivers.

1. **Globalization.** The globalization of finance has led to increased investment opportunities for hedge fund managers, a broader base of hedge fund investors, and the spread of hedge funds beyond those located solely in the West.

2. **Fund of funds (FoF).** FoF are funds that pool capital and invest that money in a variety of hedge funds, creating a portfolio of uncorrelated returns. As FoF grew in size, more capital became available to hedge funds, thus contributing to the growth of the industry. Following the 2008 financial crisis, however, the FoF industry has come under increased strain due to the reluctance of investors to pay double fees (one layer of fees charged by the FoF and a second layer of fees taken by the actual hedge fund), revelations of poor due diligence by FoF in the wake of the Bernie Madoff scandal, and perhaps most importantly, generally sub-par performance.

3. **Endowments, pensions, and foundations.** As endowments and foundations felt pressure to realize greater than anaemic returns, and pensions faced the spectre of unfunded liabilities, these institutions turned to

---

[4]Citi Investor Services, *Opportunities and Challenges for Hedge Funds in the Coming Era of Optimization, Part 1: Changes Driven by the Investor Audience,* 2014.

alternative investments such as hedge funds for both improved returns and improved stability of those returns.

David Swensen, Chief Investment Officer of the Yale University endowment since 1985, is credited with spearheading this trend. Over the last approximately 20 years, Swensen has achieved an annualized return of 14.2%, with a spectacular 21.9% return in 2011. His investment strategy has been dubbed the 'Yale Model' or 'Endowment Model' and relies heavily on investing in alternative investments (albeit with a bias towards private equity). As more endowments and pensions followed this model, more capital became available for hedge funds, spurring growth of the industry.

Hedge Fund + Commodities = Commodities Corporation

Thus far, we have introduced the founding father of hedge funds, looked at his influence on shaping the industry, discussed the definition of hedge funds, and looked briefly at how the hedge fund industry has grown. Perhaps at this point it is appropriate to briefly mention the first firm that institutionalized a hedge fund approach focused on commodities.

After writing a dissertation on the dynamics of the world's cocoa market, Helmut Weymar took his knowledge and newly bestowed PhD in economics from MIT to Nabisco. After a few years at Nabisco, Weymar – along with family friend and mentor Amos Hostetter, fellow Nabisco worker Frank Vannerson, and a group of MIT faculty members that included Nobel Prize winner Paul Samuelson, who was Weymar's PhD advisor – decided to found Commodities Corporation, a firm focused on trading commodities.

Started in 1969, Commodities Corporation became a major player initially in commodities before expanding into managed futures. After a long record of success, Commodities Corporation was bought by Goldman Sachs in 1997 and eventually incorporated into Goldman Sachs Asset Management. Besides being the forerunner of hedge funds investing significantly in commodities, perhaps Commodities Corporation's most important legacy is its record as a training ground for some of the world's most renowned hedge fund managers – including individuals such as Louis Bacon (Moore Capital Management), Paul Tudor Jones (Tudor Investment Corporation), and Bruce Kovner (Caxton Associates).

Whither Energy and Commodity Hedge Funds?

As pensions, endowments, and other pools of capital seek investment opportunities to manage unfunded liabilities related to demographic trends and capital costs, hedge funds continue to grow as an investment vehicle. There is high growth in the size of assets under management, in the diversity of strategies and products traded or invested, and in the size and geographic dispersion of the financial services industry available to serve hedge fund market participants.

Within this milieu, today's energy and commodity hedge funds, similar to Commodities Corporation before them, are sought after investment opportunities for a number of reasons, including:

- performance that is generally not correlated to equity and bond markets or the business cycle;
- their volatility and inherent opportunity set to generate performance;
- the opportunities that arise from the imperfections in the energy and commodities markets; and
- increasing liberalization of the underlying energy and commodities markets, increasing the capacity for speculative capital deployment.

Furthermore, the trend in the USA and Europe is towards increasingly deregulated, liberalized, privatized, transparent, and liquid energy markets. There is commodity convergence as well as geographic convergence – both regional and intercontinental – through linkages such as traded liquefied natural gas (LNG) and emissions allowances. The shale oil and gas 'revolution' has also driven new dynamics of supply and demand that generate new trading opportunities. These factors will continue to propel increased growth of these already substantial markets. This growth will be further stimulated by the energy and commodity needs of not just the developed world but also the increasingly important developing world.

Moving Forward

Based on the drivers described immediately above, we feel there are incredible opportunities for energy and commodity hedge funds. The purpose of this book is to highlight some of those opportunities; assist the hedge fund manager in creating a world-class firm to capitalize on these opportunities; and assist the hedge fund investor when investing in such world-class funds.

We will spend the next two chapters looking at the different primary markets that comprise the energy and commodities universe. After laying that foundation, the remainder of the book will focus on issues that are critical for hedge fund managers and hedge fund investors.

Bibliography

Berman, M. (2007) *An Introduction to Hedge Funds*. Risk Books: London.

Coggan, P. (2011) *Guide to Hedge Funds: What They Are, What They Do, Their Risks, Their Advantages (The Economist)*. John Wiley & Sons: Hoboken, NJ.

Conroy, T. (2011) Investment return of 21.9% brings Yale endowment value to $19.4 billion. *Yale News*, 28 September.

Dodd–Frank Wall Street Reform and Consumer Protection Act (2010) 12 U.S.C. § 5301.

Drobny, S. (2010) *The Invisible Hands: Top Hedge Fund Traders on Bubbles, Crashes, and Real Money*. John Wiley & Sons: Hoboken, NJ.

Drobny, S. and Ferguson, N. (2009). *Inside the House of Money, Revised and Updated: Top Hedge Fund Traders on Profiting in the Global Markets*. John Wiley & Sons: Hoboken, NJ.

Gilpin, K.N. (1997) Goldman says it will buy Asset Adviser. *New York Times*, 1 May.

Investment Advisers Act (1940) 15 U.S.C. § 80b-1.

Jones, A.W. (1949) Fashions in forecasting. *Fortune*, March, pp. 88–91, 180, 182, 184, 186.

Lack, S. (2012) *The Hedge Fund Mirage: The Illusion of Big Money and Why It's Too Good to Be True*. John Wiley & Sons: Hoboken, NJ (for a more critical view of hedge funds).

Landau, P. (1968) Alfred Winslow Jones: The long and the short of the founding father. *Institutional Investor*, August.

Landau, P. (1968) The hedge funds: Wall Street's new way to make money. *New York Magazine*, 21 October, pp. 20–24.

Lhabitant, F.S. (2006) *Handbook of Hedge Funds*. Wiley Finance Series. John Wiley & Sons: Chichester.

Loomis, C.J. (1966) The Jones nobody keeps up with. *Fortune*, April, pp. 237, 240, 242, 247.

Lowenstein, R. (2001) *When Genius Failed: The Rise and Fall of Long-Term Capital Management*. Random House: New York.

Mallaby, S. (2010) *More Money Than God: Hedge Funds and the Making of a New Elite*. Penguin Group: New York.

McDonald, D. (2007) The running of the hedgehogs. *New Yorker*, 9 April.

Rosenblum, I. (2003) *Up, Down, Up, Down, Up: My Career at Commodities Corporation*. Xlibris: Bloomington, IN.

Scaramucci, A. (2012) *The Little Book of Hedge Funds*. John Wiley & Sons: Hoboken, NJ.

SEC (2003) *Implications of the Growth of Hedge Funds: Staff Report to the United States Securities and Exchange Commission*.

Swensen, D. (2000) *Pioneering Portfolio Management: An Unconventional Approach to Institutional Investment*. Free Press: New York.

Chapter 3

What Are Energy Commodities?

*Gold and silver, like other commodities, have an
intrinsic value, which is not arbitrary, but is dependent
on their scarcity, the quantity of labour bestowed in
procuring them, and the value of the capital employed
in the mines which produce them.*
David Ricardo

Introduction

This chapter focuses on addressing two very fundamental questions for
those interested in energy commodities:

1. What are energy commodities?
2. Why are energy commodities attractive for investors?

Though multiple books could be written about various aspects of energy
commodities, we have distilled what we feel to be the key, practical nuggets
of knowledge necessary to understand the major energy commodities. The
latter half of the chapter builds on that base by looking at why this sector
might be attractive for investors.

What Are Energy Commodities?

In the aggregate, oil, coal, and natural gas (i.e., the 'Big Three') remain the
principal energy sources used by individuals and companies globally to fuel
vehicles, provide electricity, and warm homes during the winter and cool

them in the summer. Ancillary sources of energy include hydroelectricity, nuclear power, and renewable energy sources.

Oil

Owing to recent conflicts in the Middle East and catastrophic oil spills over the last few years, oil may evoke the most negative emotional response of all the energy sources. That said, oil has been a globally traded energy commodity for decades. In fact, until recently it was also the only extensively traded global energy source.

Crude oil was the first widely exchange-traded energy commodity, beginning with the launch of the West Texas Intermediate contract on the New York Mercantile Exchange in 1978. Since then, oil has continued to be actively traded and is a very liquid commodity for both hedging and speculative purposes. Alongside the trading of physical oil and its derivatives, the securities of both large and small oil companies are also actively traded. Additionally, oil has spawned other tangential industries including, most noticeably of late, 'fracking'.[5] The rise of fracking has led to a renaissance of the US energy industry, bringing the USA the closest it has been to energy independence since the mid-20th century.

Coal

Coal has for many decades been transported over great distances from mine to market. For much of this time, however, a specific generation facility was built and technically optimized to burn coal from a specific mine. The acquisition of coal was usually secured for long time periods through long-term contracts. Thus, much of the coal 'trade' consisted of predefined point-to-point logistics. This technical optimization of generation facilities to mine specific coal output was possible in a period when coal was in abundant and cheap supply and when electricity generators were largely protected monopolies with little to no cost or price sensitivity.

For much of the world, however, that time is now past. New power plant design considers coal source flexibility and emissions minimization as economically important design characteristics. Although shipping costs account for a substantial portion of coal price and its volatility, the NYMEX, ICE, and EEX exchanges all have traded coal futures contracts. Much more coal volume is traded over-the-counter (OTC). To some degree, each liberalized

---

[5]Fracking refers to hydraulic fracturing, which is a method to extract oil and natural gas by creating fractures in rocks and then increasing the size of those fractures by inserting high-pressure fluid into the openings thereby allowing oil and natural gas to escape.

coal generation facility is competing either directly or indirectly with every other facility in the world for scarce coal supplies and mine-to-market transportation capacity. As a result, demand-side factors in China or Japan, supply-side factors in South Africa or Australia, and shipping factors throughout the world can affect the price of coal delivered. In turn, this influences the economic dispatch merit order of power generation facilities throughout Europe.

Liquefied Natural Gas

Historically, LNG was sold by producers to power generation companies in conjunction with long-term requirements and contracts, much like coal. One or both contract counterparties would often build the liquefaction plant, own and operate the ships, and build and own the degasification plants. Even today, LNG producers will attempt, with decreasing levels of success, to keep LNG tankers from entering a traded market. During the last five years, there has been a growth in the number of operations which exist solely to trade LNG. Some ship-owning utilities routinely divert LNG shipments designated for their home markets to higher-priced markets elsewhere. This diversion opportunity provides a linkage, however tentative and weak, between natural gas markets in Europe, the UK, and the East and Gulf Coasts of the USA. LNG destined for Japan, Korea, or China could also end up on the West Coast of the USA, or vice versa. Indeed, after Japan's Fukushima disaster, the trend has been for Japan to be the destination of large portions of spare LNG supply. The point is that whether or not LNG is diverted, the fact that it can now be diverted impacts price and links prices across the ocean.

The Regionality of Electricity

Before moving further, it is worthwhile to share a few points about electricity. Electricity is the principal product generated by a power plant using coal, natural gas, nuclear power, or other energy commodity. Oil is generally a minor player in terms of electricity generation. Different countries and regions in the world may rely on different levels of energy commodities for their electricity needs. For example, Table 3.1 shows that coal and natural gas are the main sources of electricity generation in the USA. The distribution would look significantly different in a country like France, for instance, that relies predominantly on nuclear power for its electricity needs.

Though electricity is a product of energy commodities, electricity itself is also traded like coal, oil, and natural gas. Electricity markets are both

TABLE 3.1 2013 Electricity sources in the USA

Energy source	Percentage of total electricity generation
Coal	39%
Natural gas	27%
Nuclear	19%
Hydropower	7%
Other renewables	
Biomass	1.48%
Geothermal	0.41%
Solar	0.23%
Wind	4.13%
Petroleum	1%
Other gases	<1%

Source: US Energy Information Administration.

global and regional. They remain regional in their dynamics for a number of reasons, foremost of which is that electricity cannot be meaningfully stored, which requires the balance between power generated and power consumed to stay in balance.

First, electricity suffers from serious transmission constraints. Electricity cannot be efficiently or economically transmitted over long distances. A long-distance transmission infrastructure is incredibly expensive to build and maintain, and in addition to being costly, a large percentage of electrical energy is lost in the form of heat if transported over long distances due to electrical resistance.

Second, regional electricity markets exist due to transmission network bottlenecks. Intra-continental power pools are often connected, but transmission bottlenecks can occur as soon as contiguous-region supply or demand becomes too unbalanced.

Third, the instantaneous nature of the supply–demand relationship in electricity, and the importance of weather dynamics to electricity prices, tend to mean that regional dynamics dominate.

For all these reasons, electricity is, and is likely to remain, regional in nature, allowing for the fact that global electricity-generation fuels are playing an increasing role in regional-based pricing.

Why Are Energy Commodities Attractive for Investors?

Energy commodities are an attractive asset class because understanding them can be thought of as a complex but solvable problem, giving considerable potential returns to analysis and skill. Furthermore, although there are significant risks specific to each energy commodity market – especially extreme price volatility and physical and logistics-related event risk – much of the risk associated with these commodities is foreseeable and understandable. Such a market rewards the diligent analyst and the skilled trader with large and profitable investment opportunities.

The price development of energy commodities, especially non-crude-oil commodities, can be substantially independent of financial market behaviour and macroeconomic business cycles. Although there are occasions when systemic financial disruptions in global financial markets interject themselves into energy commodity markets, these tend to be second order and not entirely unforeseeable.

Energy commodity markets continue to grow in size (Figure 3.1) despite liquidity posting a downward correction due to the GFC.

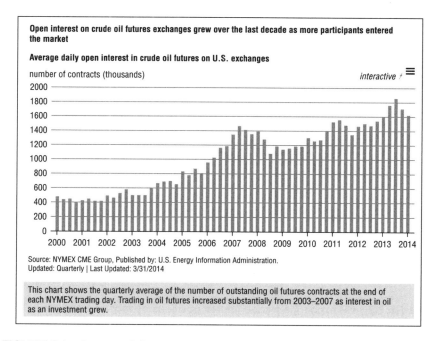

FIGURE 3.1   Average daily open interest in crude oil futures on US exchanges.

It is likely that these markets – with some exceptions – will be able to continue absorbing substantial new capital for the forseeable future. The shortage of investment skill is unlikely to disappear, especially given the growth in potentially tradable markets. At the same time, large, regionally traded portfolios of commodity products will become increasingly linked through increasingly globally traded instruments such as emissions allowances, LNG futures, coal futures, and contracts on ocean-going logistics capacity. As the BRIC (i.e., Brazil, Russia, India, and China) countries and the areas of Asia and Latin America continue to industrialize and experience significant economic growth, the demand for energy is likely to grow unabated for some time to come. The energy commodity asset class or portfolio of investable instruments is, therefore, likely to grow in size and opportunity for a period measured in decades rather than years.

The last several decades have witnessed the continuous growth of energy commodities as an investable asset class. Aside from the interest of financial markets in diversifying investment portfolios, the most important growth drivers are peculiar to the energy commodity markets themselves. These trends suggest that traded energy commodity markets may continue absorbing increasingly large amounts of capital from speculative players such as hedge funds without fear that this absorption capacity will diminish any time in the near future (Figure 3.2).

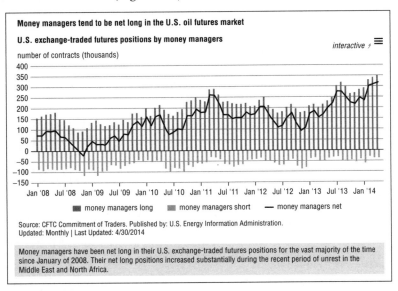

FIGURE 3.2 US exchange-traded futures positions by money managers.

To understand the growth drivers peculiar to energy commodity markets, we offer a brief and simplistic examination of the energy demand evolution that accompanies economic development. We review the most relevant drivers of energy demand evolution in developing economies, and how energy demand profiles evolve, before turning to energy market liberalization, integration, and harmonization in developed economies.

Developing Economies

The BRIC countries, together with other Asian and Latin American economies, are often-quoted examples of rapidly developing economies. With these in mind, it is useful to perform a very simplistic examination of the energy demand evolution that accompanies economic development.

Much of the dramatic growth of emerging economies can be attributed to the movement of labour from subsistence agriculture to higher economic value manufacturing. This shift is accompanied by wealth accumulation which – although miniscule on a per capita basis when compared with developed economies – stimulates demand for energy-intensive activities at both the household and national level.

Increased household wealth accumulation permits the consumption of energy beyond cooking and lighting, and introduces energy demand related to transportation, entertainment, telecommunications, and technology. For example, the impact of an extra television on the energy demand of an average Canadian household of 2.6 people, which includes 1.8 televisions already, is not marginally significant. An increase in energy demand from a household in a developing economy, however, may be driven by installing artificial lighting for the first time. This sudden and dramatic increase in the energy intensiveness of an economy has profound implications. This is compounded in cases such as China and India, where the economy involves a substantial population, vast geographic distances, and a shortage of indigenous energy supplies.

Large developing economies such as China and India have no recourse but to tap global energy markets for oil, LNG, and coal to meet the growth in energy demand. This impacts energy commodity markets globally, and alters the demand profiles of each region. China, for instance, has begun to invest considerably at home and across the Sino-Pacific region in growing its ability to access energy. Natural gas and oil pipeline projects, together with strategic rail linkages, have featured significantly in China's recent regional investment strategy. The demand for increased energy access increasingly dominates the geopolitical strategy of rapidly emerging economies.

Energy Demand Profile Evolution

As the focus of economic activity evolves from agriculture to industry to services, the structure of energy demand undergoes considerable change. While it is obvious that pre-industrial agrarian economies have both a relatively lower absolute energy demand and a relatively lower energy input per unit of economic output than industrial ones, it is less obvious that the energy demand structure changes dramatically during an economy's evolution from industrial to post-industrial. Industrial economies are often centred around several large, heavy industries that provide employment directly and indirectly to substantial portions of the population. Whether these industries involve metal smelting, chemical manufacturing, or automobile production, they are all characterized by very high energy consumption. Many national regulatory regimes have required household and commercial energy consumers to subsidize industrial energy prices based on the logic that the industrial employer requires lower energy prices to compete while the household and commercial consumers are beneficiaries of the employment created by the industrial consumer.

While large industrial centres are obvious regions of intense energy consumption, banking and financial centres are also significant energy consumers. One of the challenges that California experienced in the mid-1990s was meeting the energy requirements of the growing technology industry. In addition to the amount of energy required, consistency of supply is particularly important for tertiary sector economies. The briefest interruption can impact service companies globally, and short-term interruptions or instability can idle tens of thousands of highly paid employees.

Post-industrial, technology-intensive economies often require much greater system reliability because their demand is spread over much larger geographies and perhaps greater periods of time, which can impact peak and off-peak times for power demand. With a global rather than a local footprint, service companies cannot rely on local emergency generation plans like local heavy industries can. California provides a clear example of evolving energy demand profiles. California saw its energy intensity per unit of economic output drop considerably and its need for a stable and dependable energy supply grow dramatically.

A Complex, Solvable Problem

Energy markets are a complex yet solvable problem. We first encountered this two-pronged description of energy markets in a discussion with a fund manager of one of the world's largest and most successful energy commodity hedge funds. He was trying to decide whether the time was right to extend his fund's trading activities to Europe. To inform this decision, he was in essence trying to determine whether the European market presented: (A) a 'problem'; (B) a problem complex enough to contain trading opportunities; and (C) a problem which lent itself to solution through analysis.

Complexity is a necessary but not a sufficient condition. Solvability – whether or not the problem is solvable – is equally necessary but not sufficient. Energy commodity markets are not always complex or solvable. A market overly dominated by oligopoly producers or consumers, for instance, may be relatively simple to understand and therefore present relatively few 'problems' to be profitably solved by speculative traders.

Complexity and solvability are not necessarily related. For example, an immature energy market lacking many important 'market institutions' – such as speculative traders, regulators, exchanges, brokers, etc. – may be complex. However, it does not lend itself to being understood given the absence of institutions and the lack of levers enabling exploitation of the opportunities its complexity generates.

We agree with our fund manager friend that the energy commodity markets can be described as a highly complex yet solvable problem. Admittedly, energy commodity markets can be mind-numbingly complex, but they are also susceptible to being understood through fundamental analysis. They are a complex *and* a solvable problem, and the existence of these two necessary conditions in conjunction creates sufficient condition for investment opportunity. Below we will take a look at some of that complexity and touch on where opportunities might exist.

Drivers of Complexity

There is a diverse array of interrelated factors driving the complexity of energy markets and especially the supply, demand, and pricing of energy commodities. We will look at some of the more important drivers of energy market complexity below.

1. **Logistics.** The logistical networks associated with each of the energy commodities are inherently complex and subject to different risks, capacity constraints, and physical limitations. Most of these logistical networks – crude oil, LNG, coal, and natural gas – cover vast distances and are exposed to varying weather, regulatory, and political risks. The physical properties and transportation requirements of the various commodities

lead to usually non-interchangeable logistics networks. Each commodity has its independent network: cables and transformers for electricity, tankers for oil, freighters for coal, pipelines and compressors for natural gas, refrigerated tankers for LNG, etc. Not even the harbour facilities required for LNG, coal, and oil manipulation are interchangeable.

2. **Weather.** Logistics alone offer a vast array of complexity. Weather, however, can not only alter supply and demand, but also be a driver of logistics complexity itself. For example, electricity is often required for air conditioning in cases of high ambient temperature. At the same time, generation and transmission facilities operate at lower efficiencies in high temperatures. In some cases, the unavailability of cooling water due to higher overall temperatures will lead to generation facilities being taken off-line. This is particularly relevant for nuclear generation, where hot weather makes shutdowns a potential outcome and takes significant capacity off-line in one fell swoop. Conversely, in cases of extreme cold, natural gas is often in great demand for space heating. This makes the market value of natural gas higher in the space-heating market than in the electricity-generation fuel market. The impact of weather on emission allowances introduces yet another layer of complexity in determining the supply–demand balance for each commodity and its associated pricing.

3. **Volatility.** Largely due to logistical constraints and weather, energy markets, especially electricity markets, can be very volatile. Logistical constraints, weather, and 'cross-commodity' relationships are the prime drivers of this volatility. Additionally, unlike equity and debt instruments, the products underlying energy commodities are physical in nature and each has different physical characteristics. These physical characteristics are the source of substantial volatility. These four drivers lend themselves to deep understanding through fundamental analysis. Geopolitical and operational events, in contrast, are also important drivers of volatility but do not lend themselves easily to dependable prediction (e.g., country X cutting gas pipelines to its export markets, generator or transformer emergency shutdown, compressor station explosion, etc.). Thus, even though the nature of potential volatility-generating events may be understandable in advance, the probable impact of such events does lend itself to easy analysis.

4. **Physical characteristics.** Each energy commodity has market-relevant physical characteristics. Electricity cannot be stored (except on a small scale with capacitors) and travels at the speed of light, with the result that generation and consumption have to be virtually simultaneous for the power grid to be balanced. The opportunity for volatility-generating events is enormous. Natural gas is compressible, with the degree of

compression determined by a variety of factors including temperature. Natural gas can easily take days to travel from its production or storage location to its next storage location or final destination. The fluid dynamics associated with temperature, pressure, and infrastructure dimensions become relevant to parsing the regional supply–demand balance equation. Factors associated with the refrigeration of LNG, varying combustion dynamics of different grades, and types of coal: or physical characteristics such as these combine to make energy commodities exceedingly complex to understand.

5. **End use versatility and fungibility.** Some energy commodities are more versatile than others in that they are more fungible and there is more flexibility around their end-use applications. Natural gas can be an input into numerous production processes – it is an excellent process feedstock. For example, it can be used to produce ethylene, which is an essential building block for many chemical products. Natural gas can be burnt to generate electric power or it can be burnt for space heating. The economics of each of these uses is significantly different. Natural gas is fungible in that at any point in its logistics chain it could theoretically be diverted to any or all of the following uses: process feedstock, generation fuel, or space heating. The compressibility and storability of natural gas makes it possible to delay sales and consumption from production and acquisition as a result of analysing opportunistic economic criteria.

Crude oil can be refined into distillates ranging from gasoline and naphtha to kerosene and fuel oil. It can be burnt for either power generation or transportation (e.g., shipping). By way of contrast, although coal has end-use applications in power generation, or in the iron and steel industries (e.g., coking coal), it is fungible only to a limited degree. In fact, it is generally only fungible to some degree while still underway on a ship, barge, or train (though advances in technology may eventually change this). Once it has been unloaded, it is usually neither practical nor economically viable to divert it to different locations or uses. The refinability of various energy products into secondary products leads to tradable 'crack spreads'. This is obvious in the case of crude oil being refined into chemicals and fuels or natural gas being transformed into ethylene, but it is no less applicable to the generation of electricity from coal or natural gas for instance. The location, availability, and economics of each refinery or generation facility serve to increase the complexity of understanding cross-commodity relationships and their interlinked supply and demand curves. The ability to refine, transform, and alter the end use of energy commodities creates options that not only increase complexity, but also increase the potential return of successful fundamental analysis.

6. **Economic geography.** The economic geography of different regions leads to heterogeneous energy production, transportation, and consumption patterns. Mountainous regions often have significant hydropower generation which can be matched to electricity demand volatility. Regions historically endowed with significant lignite or hard coal deposits not only have a lignite or coal-based focus for their power-generation complexes, but also similar industrial footprints such as steel and related industries. Distance and geography dictate much about the economic feasibility and cost of building natural gas pipelines. Coal is most efficiently burned near where it is mined, but can otherwise be economically shipped only by rail or water (ocean ship or river barge). Northern regions generally have more important winter space-heating requirements, while southern regions are often more focused on air conditioning. Coastal regions are the most important direct beneficiaries of LNG, while areas with underground salt deposits can serve as natural gas and oil storage centres. Large countries such as Russia and the USA often have significant geographic heterogeneity relevant to the energy economics within their own borders. Small countries and islands such as Switzerland and the UK are often relatively homogeneous.

7. **Market liberalization.** Over the last several decades, many Western countries have largely 'liberalized' their energy markets with the result that speculative capital market participants have been able to play much larger, more diverse, and more important roles in these markets. It would be too simplistic, however, to suggest that only liberalized and integrated energy markets are attractive for energy commodity hedge funds.

    Most emerging markets are not liberalized, but their 'emerging' nature makes them quite attractive for direct or indirect market participation in some cases. On the contrary, some highly liberalized markets have become so liquid and homogeneous that investment opportunities have decreased. Some would argue, for example, that the Nordic electricity market is an example of the second category. The European Union (EU) offers an excellent study of contiguous national economies in different stages of energy market liberalization and integration. The Nordic electricity markets and the UK natural gas markets have both been widely liberalized for decades. The German electricity market is substantially liberalized, while its natural gas market has barely begun the liberalization process. In contrast, both the natural gas and electricity markets of the Netherlands are widely liberalized. The energy markets of some EU countries such as Belgium and France are largely non-liberal energy markets, and interestingly these non-liberalized markets face more significant political risks and risks from market structure due to oligopolistic or monopolistic dynamics which sometimes generate interesting opportunities if one has access to the right information. New EU entrants such as Poland, Hungary, and Romania find themselves in vastly different stages of market liberalization and integration than other EU energy markets. Electric power and natural gas regularly flow over geopolitical borders that demarcate vastly different political economic philosophies and regulatory regimes.

8. **Human capital.** Related to challenges raised during market liberalization, human capital is an often underestimated but always important driver of energy market complexity. Newly liberalized energy markets rarely have the human capital necessary to support a liquid, efficient, and growing market. The pace of trading product innovation, market structure, and regulation innovation tends to be slower than in more developed markets. The unavailability of adequately skilled and experienced human capital in sufficient numbers tends to constrain the ability of speculative capital to be widely deployed in such developing energy markets. This shortage and inexperience of human capital stock manifests itself in a markedly lower level of liquidity than might otherwise be possible.

9. **Climate change and emissions policy.** National and supranational climate change and emissions policies are increasingly linking otherwise disconnected markets – as defined both by geography and product. This results in new levels of complexity and volatility in the increasingly interlinked markets. At the launch of the European Emissions Trading Scheme (EU ETS), US gas, coal, and electricity traders were able to ignore the scheme unless they were also directly trading in the European energy commodity markets. Now, almost 10 years after the scheme commenced, many large US natural gas traders feel that they are no longer able to maintain their competitive advantage – their edge – in US natural gas markets unless they are also participating in European emissions markets.

    In the US, most electricity is generated by coal fired turbines and coal prices tend to set the floor fuel price for electricity generation. Natural gas sold into US electricity generation markets must therefore contend with the price of coal. LNG prices increasingly influence US pipeline gas prices. Since both coal and LNG have Europe and Asia as alternative market destinations, European emissions prices have an indirect but real influence on US coal and natural gas prices. As several US states and regional groups of states or municipalities begin to consider linkages with the EU ETS scheme (e.g., California), the intercontinental and cross-commodity linkages are likely to grow rather than diminish.

10. **Real and financial economy dynamics.** The maturity, traditions, and dynamics of the real and financial macroeconomy and its institutions

often impact the complexity of energy markets. Attitudes towards and experiences around financial hedging, regional economic productivity, and growth patterns all impact the deployment of financial and human capital in energy markets. A market experiencing rapid deindustrialization will probably witness a significant change in energy demand drivers.

Energy-consumption patterns associated with so-called 'industrial economies' tend to be very different from those associated with so-called 'knowledge economies'. Both have significant energy requirements with very different demand characteristics. For example, a planned, short-term interruption of electricity deliveries to an aluminium smelter driven by a high electricity price may be plausible and even net advantageous to the economy, the energy supplier, and the aluminium smelter. Interruption, for whatever reason, of the electricity supply to major computer and telecommunications centres, however, is a different story. In this case the interruption could idle thousands of employees, impairing a region's ability to make hotel and plane reservations or process insurance claims. Participants in well-developed and mature financial markets are more likely to trust and respect market mechanisms and to be more reluctant to tolerate non-market-based interventions. For example, the early days of the EU ETS witnessed several instances of dramatic and costly regulatory interference in the operation of orderly markets. The EU is currently trying to centralize control of the EU ETS to minimize the ability of individual member states to interfere in the markets to manage outcomes for national policy reasons.

Conditions for Solvability

Each of the 'drivers of complexity' briefly discussed above impacts energy markets in diverse ways, with numerous feedback effects. The high complexity of an energy market 'problem', however, is not in and of itself sufficient to make the market attractive to energy commodity hedge funds. The 'problem' must also be solvable. Numerous factors determine the solvability of the large, complex 'problem' that characterizes many energy markets. We will examine some of the core conditions for solvability below.

1. **Transparency.** The more information exists – about the market and its exchanges, production and producer operational plans, consumption and consumers, logistics and transporters – the more solvable the problem becomes. Information on clearing prices of over-the-counter

('OTC') transactions, closing prices of exchange transactions, and current pricing for transmission capacity is essential to solving the problem. Readily available meteorological information with sufficient granularity is equally important and sometimes overlooked. One meteorological data point per day, for instance, is insufficient even for a moderately sized region; a moderately sized region may have numerous energy demand-relevant microclimates. The availability, reliability, breadth, and timeliness of information distribution are all attributes of informational transparency. Transparency is a double-edged sword. It provides an edge and is the desire of every trader but it also levels the playing field. A trader's ideal scenario is informational asymmetry for everyone but him or her.

2. **Liquidity.** Market liquidity for the various tradable products in the market is essential for understanding or solving the problem because it provides information and enables market participants to act upon it. An energy market boasting an exchange with products which rarely trade or which can only be traded by a very limited population of market participants is not providing useful information. Liquid traded products reduce the uncertainty associated with pricing and volume information.

3. **Fair Market Access.** Different types of market participant may have varying levels of access to information, market exchanges, traded products, customers, counterparties, and transmission grids. These asymmetrical levels of access are usually the result of artificially imposed regulation, historical or current. Disadvantaged market participants will lack the access required for complete price discovery. Producer and consumer preferences and trade-off decisions will also be imperfect. The consequence of biased market access scenarios is an unequal playing field in solving the 'problem'. Additionally, actors will face greater uncertainty regarding the accuracy and completeness of the information inputs to any solution effort.

4. **Regulatory consistency.** There are essential market activities which should be dependable. Regulatory institutions should only intervene in normal market operations under exceptional circumstances. Furthermore, the circumstances which could give rise to intervention should be known and established in advance. To the greatest degree possible, all of the information necessary to assess the likelihood of an 'intervention scenario' should be widely known. When regulatory action vis-à-vis energy market operations and participants is transparent and consistent, it contributes to the solvability of the problem. There are very few factors capable of impairing participants' ability to understand a market more than an unpredictable and arbitrary regulator.

5. **Diversity and number of market participants.** In general, the greater the diversity and number of market participants, the more dependable and exhaustive market information becomes. Different types of market participant have different interests and perspectives: producers, hedgers, speculators, residential consumers, industrial consumers, etc. When the diversity of participants is low, information is not exhaustive. When the number of participants is low, information may in fact represent the idiosyncratic views of specific participants rather than broadly meaningful and applicable market views.

6. **Returns to skill.** We have argued that the existence of complexity surrounding the factors influencing the market for energy commodities – their pricing and trading – is not virtuous on its own. Complexity becomes a virtue only if unravelling the 'mysteries' of energy commodity markets is substantially possible through extensive analysis of the underlying physical markets. An important requirement to create a profitable trading operation, given the existence of significant non-random complexity and sufficient conditions enabling the solution of the energy market problem, is analytical skill.

The most significant component of a hedge fund manager's analytical skill is his ability to gather, integrate, and manage large amounts of market-relevant information from various sources, and to then analyse the information in a timely and accurate way to develop information-driven trading strategies. The extent to which a hedge fund manager's strategies generate returns that exceed average market returns is a measure of his skill. In financial jargon, 'alpha' represents these idiosyncratic returns – returns peculiar to a specific manager and attributable to his skill. The key component of skill in the energy commodity market is adequate and timely analysis of the myriad of factors determining energy pricing.

For example, any energy trader reads daily weather forecasts and trades based on their predictions. The best energy traders, however, have their own meteorologists who are familiar with the various models that underlie the most commonly published forecasts. A deeper understanding of periodic correlations in weather behaviour, which are not explicitly described in published forecasts, can give a trader a valuable edge. Forecasts are an excellent example of the returns to analytical skill because they are by definition an amalgamation of various potential scenarios. Each scenario is associated with different probabilities of occurring, and all are incredibly sensitive to the measurement of the initial values entered in the forecasting models. On occasion, a forecast hides two equally likely yet very different scenarios. The trader who understands the information that lies behind the forecast is better able to position his portfolio to guard against risks or exploit opportunities not seen by the casual forecast reader.

CASE STUDY

In the first half of 2007, many European energy traders followed the EU ETS emissions allowances analysis published by one of the most prominent information service providers in that new area of trading. Unfortunately, the analysis was wrong. Traders who based their strategy primarily on this one set of erroneous analysis collectively lost hundreds of millions of euros over a matter of weeks. Conversely, a few trading groups got it right. The edge that helped them get it right was proprietary, bottom-up analysis of emissions and allowances on a country-by-country and emitter-by-emitter basis.

Whether it is weather forecasting, emissions allowances, power plant availabilities and outages, or harbour bottlenecks, the deep and effective analysis of energy commodities can generate real value which translates into alpha. Although there are numerous subscription publications and services pertinent to each commodity in each region, the best analysis is often proprietary. The reason energy commodities are particularly attractive to investors is because their trading and pricing are a complex but solvable problem, and they provide real opportunities for returns to skill.

Principal Sources of Opportunity and Risk

Having viewed energy commodities as a complex, solvable problem, we now turn our attention to opportunities and risks that arise from the unique nature of energy commodities.

1. **Supply, demand, and merit order.** The investable dynamics of electricity markets are mainly its volatility, price direction, and demand direction. These are primarily functions of the supply–demand balance, which is primarily driven by weather and the dynamics that dictate how each particular fuel market responds to weather changes. Two ways in which weather can impact markets indirectly are in efficiency and operational terms. First, it can reduce the efficiency of generation and interconnect hardware. Second, it can reduce the availability of adequate volumes of cooling water at the right temperature – often requiring power plants to be taken off-line. Market dynamics in response to weather changes are often different for each electricity-generation fuel. For instance, in regions with substantial natural gas generation, weather-driven demand for natural gas (e.g., space heating) drives demand for natural gas in ways somewhat independent of electricity. This is because natural gas is

fungible to the extent that once it is in a pipeline system it can be directed to electric power generation or space heating. In areas with significant gas-fired space heating, extreme cold temperatures initially often have a greater upward impact on gas prices than on electricity prices. Gas is then diverted from the electricity generation fuel market to the heating market, which changes the supply–demand balance in other generation fuel markets such as coal. This changing 'ranking' of the economically optimal uses of different fuels as a result of weather changes and peculiar market dynamics is known as the power generation 'merit order'.

Merit order refers to the marginal cost of different generation facilities ranked by their increasing marginal cost. At any moment, the marginal cost of a specific generation facility is driven by both factors inherent to the efficiency with which that facility converts fuel to electricity and the price of the relevant fuel. In other words, the merit order is itself dynamic. The merit order dictates the size and nature of trading opportunities.

With the advent of traded emissions allowances, an additional factor has been introduced into marginal cost computations and merit order ranking. For example, reduced cooling water in the summer can result in a reduction of on-line nuclear power generation, which in turn raises the merit order of coal and implicitly the price of coal. At the same time, however, coal generation results in CO_2 emissions and requires emission allowances – unlike nuclear generation. Thus, there is a second-order feedback effect. Reduced cooling water leads to reduced availability of nuclear-powered generation, which increases demand for coal-fired generation. In turn, demand for coal increases the price of coal and simultaneously increases the demand for and price of emissions allowances. The more elevated emission allowances price ultimately increases the marginal cost of generation, coming full circle and establishing a link between weather, emission allowance cost, and merit order.

2. **Correlation.** There is such a vast amount of capital invested in different equity or bond-based investment strategies that the substantial return correlation of similar strategies and portfolios is not surprising. In fact, these returns are often significantly correlated to a small number of macroeconomic factors such as interest rates, and business cycle metrics as well as market indices. As a result, portfolio managers often find it difficult to develop a truly diversified portfolio – a portfolio made up of several dozen highly correlated investment products is not a diversified portfolio.

Energy commodities are correlated to certain factors as well, but these factors are rarely the same factors driving equity and bond market pricing. Weather, intercontinental macroeconomic factors, and logistics are likely to have a far greater impact on energy commodity prices than interest rates, equity market indices, and business cycle-related statistics. While in a macro sense there is less overall electricity demand in periods of reduced economic activity, the most important investable market dynamics of electricity are independent of the business cycle phenomena. While it is true that in any discrete location energy demand tends to be higher when economic activity is higher, the impact of weather, logistics, and substitute energy sources tends to be far more important in driving price levels. Consequently, it is fair to say that energy prices tend to be generally uncorrelated to equity and bond market performance and largely uncorrelated to business cycle-driven factors.

3. **Market liberalization, integration, and harmonization.** Market liberalization, integration, and harmonization all provide opportunities for investors in energy commodities. The process of liberalization breaks down the monopolistic or oligopolistic structures of energy producers and distributors. New legislation and regulation is implemented to eliminate market structures which create and protect monopoly power. Ironically, such structures usually exist as the result of the historical regulation that originally enabled their establishment. In order for liberalizing legislation to be effective, new market participants must be encouraged to enter the market, and they must be included in such a way that they are able to share in the risks and rewards of the market. These new market participants usually include financial investors (particularly investment banks and hedge funds), energy exchanges and brokers, and energy traders (such as those working in banks and utilities). Attracting these new market participants depends on fair market access, market transparency, and fair market regulation. Price volatility and tradable energy products – such as standardized futures and forward contracts or brokered products – will inevitably emerge in liberalizing markets. The result of a successful programme of energy market liberalization is price and service competition.

As neighbouring countries liberalize, wholesale commodity markets[6] and related logistics markets inevitably evolve and expand, leading to market integration. Long-distance natural gas pipelines tend to cross many different legal jurisdictions. Electricity is not efficiently transmitted over long distances, increasing linkages between neighbouring markets regardless of political jurisdiction. The physical laws governing electricity do not respect political borders and will follow the path to their intended destination across them if transmission linkages exist.

---

[6]We distinguish here between wholesale markets (those which are traded) and consumer retail markets.

Because of the politically charged nature of energy markets, energy transmission bottlenecks are often found at political borders prior to liberalization.

The drive for efficiency and new economic opportunities created by energy market liberalization tend to encourage infrastructure construction to minimize such bottlenecks. The result is increased market integration that will often link geographic regions with very different energy-production footprints, demand characteristics, and market dynamics. For example, the efficient linkage of hydropower-heavy regions, such as the Swiss and Austrian Alps, with nuclear power generation-heavy regions, such as France or Southern Germany, creates dramatically different economic dispatch merit orders in both markets. Baseload nuclear power generation coupled with hydropower peaking creates a more efficient portfolio of economically dispatchable energy assets.

The age and efficiency of energy infrastructure in neighbouring regions often differs significantly as well, with implications for the marginal cost of energy production and transmission. As part of the expansion of the EU, for example, contiguous energy markets such as Poland and Germany suddenly became routine energy-trading partners. Historical investment patterns in the German power-generation industry, however, are very different from Polish ones – technical plant efficiencies are much lower in Poland. Additionally, Polish power generation is overwhelmingly coal based – both lignite and hard coal – making it subject to strict emission-allowance requirements. An ageing Polish hard-coal power-generation facility in a market with rapidly rising hard-coal prices and rising emissions-certificate prices is significantly disadvantaged in relation to far more efficient German generation with significantly lower emissions – both characteristics the result of substantially greater recent investment. The integration of contiguous liberalizing energy markets is a long-term process creating sizeable microeconomic trading opportunities.

Integrating and liberalizing markets with different political and regulatory histories must inevitably contend with a challenging period of market harmonization. Each country, and sometimes each state or province, has its own economic and political interests which have created, over decades, idiosyncratic regulatory regimes. Such regimes become self-sustaining as interest groups organize to lobby and protect the market structure status quo. As neighbouring markets integrate, inconsistent regulatory regimes bring about inefficient market economic behaviour. Traders and other market participants exploit 'regulatory arbitrage' opportunities that are individually profitable to them, but frequently inefficient from a market point of view. Although the absurdities that often result from such inconsistent regulatory regimes may be quite obvious and the resulting economic inefficiency substantial, harmonizing the regulatory regimes is usually a time-consuming process involving considerable compromise that rarely results quickly in an efficient and level market playing field.

For example, in the USA substantial portions of the natural gas industry are subject to federal regulation. Additionally, state regulation of natural gas pipelines also exists, creating a complicated mosaic of regulation dependent on geography. The electric power industry, however, was primarily subject to state regulation, and was divided into nine regions that together made up the North American Electricity Reliability Counsel. Each state had its own electricity regulatory regime, and each reliability region had further region-specific rules. The federal government often set out conflicting regulations governing interstate and interregional power transmission. As a result, major bottlenecks can still be found between some regions to this day. Differences in state, regional, and federal regulation contributed significantly to the electricity shortages, brownouts, and blackouts in California in the 1990s.

Europe offers many examples of harmonization as disparate national regulatory regimes are slowly – and often reluctantly – integrated into one EU-wide regulatory framework. The UK had liberalized its largely state-owned, 'national champion' energy companies early in its drive to liberalize its electricity and natural gas markets. France and Belgium worked to protect their 'national champion' energy utilities, while Germany facilitated mergers among German utilities to create its own 'national champions'. Most EU countries implemented the initial phases of the EU ETS with regulations clearly designed to benefit their own national utilities and not to reduce emissions. EU harmonizing directives, including the implementation of the EU ETS, have regularly been met with national objections driven by vested interests. Much progress towards integration and harmonization has been made, but the pace has been predictably slow.

Liberalization opens up new markets to financial capital. Integration of markets and infrastructure connects isolated pools of trading liquidity. Combined, growing liberalization and deepening integration generates many tradable market anomalies along the way. This is particularly the case in scenarios of incomplete regulatory harmonization. Hedge funds and other trading groups will be able to continue exploiting trading opportunities for many years to come.

4. **Global capital market integration.** Having surveyed examples of scarcity as a driver of energy commodity market globalization, and seen examples of globalizing energy products, we turn to the remaining drivers: global capital market integration, increasing coverage of investors, energy exchange integration with supranational instruments, and the creation of supranational service providers.

An extensive literature is available on the subject of global capital market integration. Global investment banks rotate trading books from Singapore or Hong Kong to London, and from London to New York, before returning to Asia – the sun never sets on their open positions. This has long been true for foreign exchange and crude oil, but is increasingly true for other energy commodity products. In 2007, British and European natural gas traders began to observe significant participation of US-based traders in their markets. One prominent European natural gas trader has remarked that 2007 trading volume doubled versus 2006. More revealingly, trading dynamics changed radically as North American traders began taking positions guided less by carefully evaluated European market fundamentals and more by technical signals.

Global investors such as large hedge funds and investment banks are having a dramatic impact on the globalization of energy commodity markets. Global investors are better able to observe and exploit growing linkages between different products and geographic markets. Furthermore, the global experience of such investors serves as an institutional memory on which to draw when familiar trading patterns appear in new markets. Global investors tend to do business with many of their counterparties in multiple regions. For example, a large hedge fund trading with an investment bank in Europe is likely to also trade with that investment bank in North America and in Asia. This contributes to rapidly increasing market liquidity. Liberalization of markets and technological advances in trading platforms and communications has enabled investors to become global in their trading of energy commodities. Global investors have also driven global standards in the markets. Exchange and OTC-traded product specifications, ISDA terms, credit terms, margin requirements, and risk management standards have all been driven by global investors. One could argue that the economic efficiency gains have been considerable; investors with trading positions circling the globe help ensure that energy resources reach the markets in which they are most valued.

It is no accident that existing energy exchanges are consolidating and new energy exchanges are being launched across the world. Global financial investors find exchange-traded environments provide easy, fast, safe, and efficient market access. Exchange-traded products tend to be more easily valued for 'mark-to-market' as well as risk management purposes. Once energy exchanges in a discrete market become well established and liquid, there is a tendency towards mergers and cooperation between exchanges. In search of new revenue, exchanges tend to develop products that compete with existing products on other exchanges. This leads to the appearance of global products. Ultimately, global investors and OTC brokers tend to exert significant competitive pressure on exchanges such that mergers into increasingly larger exchanges are inevitable. Examples of this trend include the 2002 merger between the Leipzig Power Exchange (LPX) and the European Energy Exchange (EEX), and the existing close cooperation and cross-shareholding between the NordPool Exchange and the EEX.

Global investors and global market channels – brokers and exchanges – often create demand for other supranational market institutions. Global investors tend to work with many of the same large execution brokers throughout the world, and their business is split across numerous exchanges. The result is a cycle of competition for value, speed, and quality of product innovation among execution brokers and exchanges. Furthermore, exchanges indirectly foster strong market institutions – including OTC brokers, market information providers, and risk management providers. Prime brokers serving energy commodity hedge funds often seek to be single-source service providers and provide access to energy commodity markets throughout the world. Similarly, global investors grow accustomed to certain high standards of information such as daily market newsletters and real-time information service providers. Pricing feeds and risk management modelling service providers seek to provide global investors with worldwide coverage.

The impact of these trends on global commodity markets is primarily reflected in increased market liquidity, increased speed of information and product knowledge sharing, and lower volatility (until recently at least). Underlying these three trends is an increase in the interconnectedness of markets. Global investors tend to strengthen product price linkages. The link between pipeline gas and fuel gas prices in the USA and the UK, for example, has grown given the influence of LNG prices and the price of emissions allowances and traded coal prices on truly global trading positions. The increase in speculative capital deployed by global investors in energy commodity markets will tend to strengthen global price linkages. Some globally active hedge funds and investment banks also control their own proprietary private equity funds, which sometimes invest in energy-related assets that give the investor greater flexibility in global markets. These assets may include LNG tankers or coal freighters, natural gas storage facilities, or emissions remediation projects.

Bibliography

Downey, M.P. (2012) *Oil 101*. Wooden Table Press: New York.

Gold, R. (2014) *The Boom: How Fracking Ignited the American Energy Revolution and Changed the World*. Simon & Schuster: New York.

Inkpen, A. and Moffett, M.M. (2011) *The Global Oil and Gas Industry: Management, Strategy, and Finance*. PennWell Books: Tulsa, OK.

Mokhatab, S., Mak, J.Y., *et al.* (2013) *Handbook of Liquefied Natural Gas*. Gulf Professional Publishing: Houston, TX.

Raymond, M.S. and Leffler, W.L. (2005) *Oil and Gas Production in Non-Technical Language*. PennWell Books: Tulsa, OK.

Taulli, T. (2011) *All About Commodities*. McGraw-Hill: New York.

Chapter 4

Trading and Investing in Energy Commodities

Successful investing is anticipating the anticipations of others.
John Maynard Keynes

Our previous chapter identified the complexity and volatility of energy commodities as a substantial source of their attractiveness as an investment class. In a nutshell, the complexity and price volatility of energy commodities are tied directly to the physical characteristics of the commodities themselves. In particular, the physical characteristics involved in energy production and logistics are particularly important in understanding the trading dynamics of these commodities.

In order to better understand investing in energy commodities and energy commodity hedge funds, we take a slight detour to emphasize a crucial point. From an activity-based point of view, we separate a hedge fund into two components with distinctly different functions.

The first is the trading operation, which includes all those tasks that are directly related to the trading of the portfolio (i.e., portfolio management) and investment strategy design, trading strategy, market research, market analysis, and execution of trades. In this book, the trading operation will be interchangeably referred to as portfolio management, the fund, or fund management as they are often used interchangeably in the vernacular and popular press. That said, it is important to remember that legally, portfolio management activities are handled by the investment manager (or delegated to an investment advisor) on behalf of the fund. The details of legal roles and responsibilities are explained in a fund's private placement memorandum, which is explained in further detail in Chapter 6.

The second is the business management function, which covers all operational activities not directly related to portfolio management. Some of these tasks include: business strategy development, tax, legal and regulatory affairs, cash-flow planning, human resource management including recruiting, service provider and contract administration, and investor relations and fundraising. The business management function will generally be referred to in this book in the context of the firm (as opposed to the fund, which as mentioned above focuses on the investing and portfolio management aspect of a hedge fund). This chapter focuses on the portfolio management component of an energy commodity hedge fund.

An energy commodity trader can trade at a desk in a bank, at a utility, or at someone else's hedge fund or trading company. Many traders, however, might consider an option not on this list as the most desirable one – launching an energy commodity hedge fund of their own. What most traders fail to appreciate fully is that in the latter option, investment strategy becomes just as important as trading strategy.

Let us clearly define the difference between investment strategy and trading strategy. By investment strategy we mean the macro-level, overarching strategy of a fund, basically its *raison d'être*. Investment strategy is designed with a time horizon of many years in mind. By trading strategy we mean the micro-level trading approach of a fund, its short-term trading rationale, its view on the market which dictates trading positions. Trading strategy is designed for the day, the week, and the next few quarters ahead in mind.

Bottom-up and Top-down

The two main elements of investment strategy design involve selecting the markets the fund will operate in and the products the fund will build its portfolio with. These two decisions are not to be made sequentially, but in parallel, and the strategic analysis involved in the decision-making process must be forward looking – it must make allowances for the evolving nature of the fund as it matures.

In this chapter, we will approach investment strategy design through the consideration of start-up and early-stage hedge funds. Much of the same thought process is equally applicable to well-established hedge funds, but the concept and process of investment strategy design is most intuitively discussed and explained with reference to start-up or early-stage hedge funds. Many mature and successful hedge funds seem at times to be purely opportunistic with respect to the evolution of their investment strategy, as opposed to using an ongoing and consistent approach to investment strategy development. We have observed that some large hedge funds with long track records lose sight of the core investment strategy of their fund, leading to a decline in returns or a failure of off-shoot funds. The investment strategy design and development is based on our experience with both early-stage and mature hedge funds.

This chapter is written mainly from the point of view of the existing or would-be hedge fund manager, however, it is equally relevant to those who invest in commodities hedge funds. Investors should understand what considerations determine a fund's investment strategy – they will then be able to assess whether the value proposition of a fund is sustainable in the long term. In selecting funds, this understanding will enable investors to identify whether a prospective fund manager should return to the trading desk he or she came from, or help investors determine the potential size of initial and subsequent investments in those who pass the test. Additionally, it will help investors judge whether a string of good performance data is the result of luck or of carefully planned and diligently executed investment and trading strategy. Investors should ensure that a fund manager is consistently mindful of both short-term trading strategy and long-term investment strategy.

It is important that a fund manager thinks strategically about the development of the hedge fund's investment exposures because energy commodity markets can change significantly over a period of two to three years. A fund manager who is not planning ahead as these markets develop is likely to have a brief period of excellent performance followed by a long and frustrating decline when the trading and portfolio strategies of yesterday become increasingly out of date. Given the liquidity restrictions associated with energy investing, strategic investment planning in terms of market coverage and portfolio design is of equal importance. The catalogue of considerations we review in this chapter in selecting target markets and designing the hedge fund portfolio will serve would-be fund managers and investors in hedge funds alike.

We start by examining the two functional components of a hedge fund: the trading operation and the fund management business. Then we tackle a fundamental question that drives the thinking around the objectives of the fund – what is our edge?

Trading + Managing a Business = Successful Hedge Fund

There is an important distinction to make between hedge funds as a trading operation and hedge funds as a business. It is a frequently repeated statistic (perhaps apocryphal but one which we are partial to) that half of all start-up hedge funds fail during their first year of operation and more than half of those failures are attributable to operational failure rather than unsuccessful trading strategies. Operational failure includes events such as: risk management failure, bankruptcy due to no liquidity, regulatory non-compliance, money laundering, tax fraud, and many others – whether intentional or not.

In general, a trader's scope is limited to trading strategy and execution as well as limited middle and back-office activities necessary to facilitate execution. This reflects the tendency of banks, large physical merchants, large hedge funds, or commodity-producer trading operations to insulate traders from all non-market-facing, non-transaction-oriented activities, enabling complete focus on trading.

The functions performed by the trading operation of a fund are pretty much the only functions a trader at a bank or trading house is generally exposed to. They include only tasks that are directly related to trading: investment research, investment analysis, trade execution, and trade settlement. Almost logically then, when bank or utility traders decide to launch their own hedge funds, they often underestimate the resources and planning required for the many aspects of managing a business.

The business of managing an investment firm includes such varied activities as paying the light bill or managing payroll administration as well as a host of other factors. The trader on the bank trading floor who thought these functions were bureaucratic distractions suddenly discovers their importance when running his own fund. This discovery, however, frequently takes place too late, after having ignored the business until the office rent is overdue, profits disappear into unanticipated taxes, or employees fail to get paid. Many well-compensated, senior-ranked traders on the trading floor have little concept of the components or need for non-market-facing business management.

An aspiring fund manager must commit to both trading well and managing well. Only focusing on one without paying attention to the other will ultimately lead to failure. There are methods to make sure both trading and managing functions are taken care of, which are discussed throughout this book. At a very basic level, a fund manager must accept responsibility for the fund's performance as well as the integrity of its ongoing management.

The Edge?

A key starting point for our market selection and portfolio analysis is to determine what makes a fund unique. Tackling this fundamental question enables the fund manager to start with tangible objectives in mind that shape the design of the trading operation to chosen markets and strategies. We sum this point up by asking the question: What is our edge? Or posed another way:

- What is the source of alpha?
- Is the alpha-generating competitive advantage sustainable?
- What will an investor get from investing in this fund manager that he or she cannot get from investing in an index or other passive exposure instrument of these markets?

Trading is sometimes viewed as a straightforward maximization exercise (i.e., maximizing absolute returns and minimizing risk). When aiming to establish and grow a trading business, however, one must consider the complete trading strategy. All too often traders turned fund managers replace the big picture of analysis with an excessive focus on the trading itself. Upfront decisions will be required not only for marketing purposes, but also to help plan the business venture.

Initially one must ask: what will be our unique, sustainable, competitive advantage? What is our edge? If there is a clearly distinguishable track record, one must identify past reasons for good and bad performance. There are three key issues to consider.

First, the reason behind good (or bad) performance could be dependent on the future portfolio manager's former seat (in terms of informational advantage that is a function of his or her role), or his or her former team. One or both of these may not follow the trader to the new hedge fund. The potential downside of leaving this seat and team behind should be considered by both fund manager and investor. Additionally, it is critical to remember that performance numbers alone do not reveal the whole story of a portfolio manager's performance. Such performance numbers must be considered in the context of contemporaneous risk parameters that the portfolio manager was guided by when managing the portfolio being reviewed.

Second, the portfolio of counterparties and associated credit terms may become an issue, since they are unlikely to be available in the early stages of the fund.

Third, the organizational infrastructure going forward must be evaluated. If the trader is leaving a big bank or institutional investor, it is unlikely that much of that infrastructure will be replicated in the firm in the near to medium term.

Beyond the top-down approach of establishing the competitive advantage and exploiting it, a bottom-up approach is also required. This lies in evaluating the market in which the fund will play. The trading strategy must ask: to what products and geographies do target investors want exposure?

The start-up or early-stage fund manager almost always starts his business strategy with a focus on the products which he has the greatest experience with. For many hedge funds the entire strategy can be deduced from the CVs of the team that will comprise the portfolio trading staff. Nevertheless, this is an inadequate basis for determining the strategy of the firm and its constituent funds or portfolios. The initial inputs to the process of determining the optimum playing field in terms of product and geography will of necessity include the experience of the would-be fund manager him/herself as well as his/her planned team. Though the experiences of the would-be fund manager are important, the interests of potential investors are also significant. Investors know that traders like to 'talk their own book'. A rigorous investment analyst is interested in understanding not only the trading strategy and products but also why the market or markets are interesting. Europe offers an excellent example.

The NordPool electricity markets of Norway and Sweden were liberalized well before other European power markets. Not surprisingly, there are a large number of experienced NordPool traders who would consider launching hedge funds. Many investors, however, perceive that the Nord-Pool market alone offers too much risk for too little return and that there are few truly excellent traders in that market. Investors are often looking for Germany-focused strategies that can also trade the Nordic markets as relative value plays and for portfolio diversification.

Here we find at least four aspects of strategy: (1) the core competence of the fund manager; (2) the interests of the investors; (3) the possible construction of a portfolio with an attractive risk–reward profile; and (4) the availability of additional intellectual capital to exploit additional strategies.

The characteristics of certain products (e.g., regional vs. global) and of certain investor portfolios suggest that the geographic coverage of the fund – including limiting it – is important. For example, a US natural gas hedge fund manager suggests that because of increasing correlation between US and UK natural gas, it will be necessary to trade both to be an effective investor in the US natural gas market. For a US natural gas trader, trading UK natural gas inherently implies a trading presence on a different continent in a different time zone and under a different regulatory regime. Clearly, the portfolio risk–reward features associated with the multi-continent strategy must be balanced by the increase in operational risk and management distraction. These are the types of consideration that go into developing good fund management company business strategy.

Trading Energy Commodities

At a high level, trading energy commodities can be divided into trading the physical and trading the financial derivative of the physical commodity. For example, an oil trader for an industrial or manufacturing company might actually trade barrels of oil with the intention of his company taking physical delivery of those barrels of oil in order to use the oil as input in their value chain to create a product. This simple example represents a trader involved in trading the physical commodity.

In contrast, a trader that is trading an option, future, or other derivative where the underlying component of the derivative is an energy commodity such as oil is said to be trading the financial derivative of the physical commodity. In this situation, the trader generally does not want to take physical delivery of the commodity but is either hedging or speculating using derivatives based on volatility, price, or other factors. Most of the traders that we think about in this book are generally traders who are involved in this type of activity.

Quite often it is a different group of traders that dominate the physical markets vs. the financial markets – the former being dominated by physical trading houses such as Glencore, utilities in their hedging capacity, and other energy companies; the latter often being dominated by the speculative capital of banks (less and less given increasing regulation of the banking sector), hedge funds, and the proprietary desks of utility trading divisions. But the physical market's evolution, and the evolution of its regulation, investment in its infrastructure, and even the perceived preference of its products (e.g., gas vs. coal, LNG, etc.) is not at all independent of the speculative capital markets whose direct investments may tend to be more focused on the financial markets. While no trader would expect the markets to be unrelated, energy executives and regulators often ignore or underestimate the importance of speculative capital in commodity markets. At the same time, financial speculators have often underestimated the importance of active involvement in the regulatory evolution of the physical markets.

We will highlight here the impact of speculative capital markets on the operation, regulation, investment, and development of the physical underlying markets. Additionally, we will explore the evolution of financial institutions including exchanges, brokers, clearing houses, regulators, and banks in response to the growth of speculative capital in these markets. The impact on service providers – both to the energy industry and to the energy commodity-related capital markets – continues to evolve in response to the increasing presence and dynamism of speculative capital in these markets.

As with most markets, almost all energy markets in the world are regulated. Deregulated or liberalized markets are regulated in the sense that they have become differently regulated from what they were in the past. In more mature liberal markets, greater losses or gains are often made by speculative market participants than by the relevant underlying energy industry participants. The brief but spectacular collapse of Amaranth and the economic catastrophe of trader-induced chaos in the California power markets are but two examples of the important connections between speculative capital markets and the markets of the physical underlying.

As investors evaluate fund managers as well as the suitability of markets for hedge fund trading they must be aware of the 'feedback loops' between the largely financial speculative capital energy markets and the largely physical markets of the underlying. Investors, fund managers, and service providers should be active participants in the political and regulatory processes that give shape to the evolution of these markets. Energy executives and investors in energy companies, including utilities, dare not ignore the development of speculative capital markets as they strategize or evaluate the strategies of the companies in which they invest.

For example, if large amounts of risk capital are trading in German power and emissions, what does that do in the 'real world' of electricity users, generators, transporters, etc.? There is a real impact due to this activity and regulators should be interested. In another example, investors long on emissions drove up emissions prices, which drove up electricity prices that German utilities pushed through to their small commercial and household customers through regulated rate increases. Through their trading arms, utilities were frequently able to benefit from this trading activity, which began in the financial markets but ultimately disadvantaged everyday consumers. Regulators and government policymakers must consider the speculative markets when designing regulation, rate design, and other market structures that shape the energy commodity markets.

Additionally, utility strategists cannot ignore speculative markets. They must either actively participate as traders or find a way to hedge themselves. Some large ones – such as RWE and EDF – have developed substantial competence in energy trading, while other firms such as E.ON seem to have decided they will not and expose themselves to that potential market risk.

In the previous chapter, we highlighted principal energy commodities such as electricity, natural gas, coal, and oil industries along with their respective logistics value chains. Much of the dramatic volatility associated with natural gas and electric power markets derives from logistics constraints and weather variability. Additionally, the complexity of regulations when it comes to power, which is compounded by multiple jurisdictions and agencies that might be involved in such regulation, creates a complexity that offers potentially attractive returns to deep research and analysis as well as trading skill. The volatility – though often extreme – is not random. It is understandable and often predictable. Each of these energy and related commodities has its own set of supply and demand drivers for price, logistics capacity, and physical commodity. Nonetheless, there is enough interconnectedness in the supply–demand drivers (e.g., weather) to potentially predict price volatility and some extreme events (or at least foresee them as a reasonably likely possibility). These features of the energy and related commodities will be explored at some depth, allowing the reader to understand the great potential for 'alpha' and uncorrelated return generation in these markets.

For the investor new to these markets, beyond the economics there are also unique political and regulatory environments of the commodities to consider. Whereas a brief delay in the delivery of coffee beans or newsprint might cause a temporary price spike and a logistics log-jam in certain industries, a brief delay in the delivery of electricity or natural gas can cause shutdowns of entire industries and blackouts, leading to an associated crime increase in major metropolitan areas or the death of vulnerable citizens due to interrupted air conditioning or heating. The financial investor cannot afford to ignore the very real possibility of *force majeure* events resulting from threats to human life and safety, property, or economic activity.

Basic Financial Knowledge for Commodities

There are some key concepts and themes that one must know to begin understanding energy commodities. We will highlight a few of the key principles in this section.

When thinking about commodities, a foundational concept is that they are intrinsically different from investing in an asset class like equities or bonds. The same factors that drive equities and bonds will affect commodities differently. For example, commodities are generally positively correlated with inflation, while stocks and bonds are generally negatively correlated with commodities. Additionally, since stocks and bonds are driven by calculating a revenue stream or cash flow, their pricing is very much forward looking, while commodity pricing tends to more directly reflect the immediate to near-term situation.

The basic underlying framework of commodity investing revolves around forward or future contracts and statistical jargon. Forward contracts and future contracts are essentially the same thing. Each is a contractual promise to deliver a certain quantity of a certain item at a specified time at a specified price. People can enter into these contracts to lock in prices if they are afraid the price of a particular item may increase in the future or if they want certainty in budgeting. They can also be used for speculative purposes. For example if an investor believes the current price of something they own will decrease in the future and they would like to lock in a guaranteed price now in case there is depreciation. The difference between a forward and a future is that a future is traded on an exchange, while a forward is not and is usually privately negotiated between counterparties.

Energy commodity traders may use a future or other derivative to take a view on a particular commodity; however, the basics of futures pricing underpin many of the different products that a trader may use. For example, any sort of swap product that a trader uses can be viewed as a series of forward contracts put together into one derivative.

As forward contracts are operative for different lengths of time before they expire, there is a particular vernacular that is used to signal if a contract is expiring sooner or if it is expiring later. For example, if an investor is viewing two futures contracts, the contract closest to expiry is the *nearby contract* while the contract that has more time to expiry is the *deferred contract*. This distinction is important to remember as it exemplifies the principle of the *term structure of forward prices*. The term structure of forward prices represents the relationship between the price of the forward and the time of delivery for that forward. This pattern of price and time makes sense if we use a basic real-world example. During the summer months in Arizona, more people are using their electricity to power their air conditioners because of the heat. The forward price of electricity will reflect this cyclical pattern of price and time. This relationship is captured in the term structure of forward prices.

Perhaps the last piece of basic information to cover is the jargon that is used to discuss commodity pricing. Traders or people involved in the markets frequently use the words 'contango' or 'backwardation'. These words are simply adjectives to describe a particular situation. Neither contango nor backwardation is inherently bad or good, they are just terms that capture the current market.

When a market is in contango, this refers to situations where the futures price exceeds the expected future spot price. Conversely, a market is in backwardation when the futures price is lower than the expected future spot. For a visual image of both contango and backwardation, see Figure 4.1.

Conclusion

This particular chapter on trading and investing in energy commodities could easily have been a book in its own right, and indeed many books have been written on the topic. This chapter was written with two groups in mind: (1) traders who know the technical aspects of trading energy commodities very well but may not understand the investment mindset of asset allocators; and (2) asset allocators and other investment professionals who

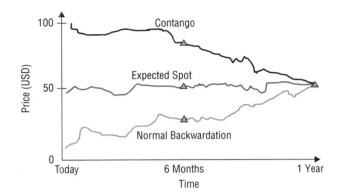

FIGURE 4.1   A visual image of contango and backwardation.
Source: Stable Asset Management.

may not be experts in energy commodities but need to know the basics to understand some of the tools and jargon that is used by fund managers trading energy commodities.

With the idea of continuing these themes, we have included a checklist for both groups that will help you think through the different issues and constraints you may face when thinking about starting a new hedge fund or when considering where to allocate capital to such an endeavour.

Checklist for the fund manager:

- ☐ In which commodities (products) do you wish to trade?
- ☐ In which markets (geographically)?
- ☐ In what form (financial: futures, options, swaps; and/or physical)?
- ☐ Via what channels (exchanges, execution brokers, banks, physical market counterparties)?
- ☐ With what market risk profile?
- ☐ Employing what types of trading strategy?
- ☐ With what return and portfolio risk expectations?
- ☐ With what capital deployment limitations?
- ☐ With what regulatory constraints?
- ☐ In what markets will the fund be marketed?
- ☐ Trading strategy: structure-relevant strategy issues include exchange traded vs. OTC, leverage and physical trading, etc.
- ☐ Trading platforms: exchanges, financial brokers, OTC banks, OTC utilities, and physical counterparties, etc.

☐ What risk management parameters will exist based on tools such as maximum single-day stress test, margin-to-equity ratio, value at risk, etc.?

☐ What assets under management (AUM) can a fund safely deploy in the market with what level of expected drawdown?

☐ Adding certain products and/or geographies increases the possibility for relative value positions instead of purely directional positions. Will this contribute to greater AUM? Will risk increase?

Checklist for an investor contemplating investing in an energy commodity hedge fund:

☐ Does the fund manager have a proven track record?
  ☐ It should not be enough for a start-up or early-stage manager to show a track record, especially if that track record is not demonstrably connected to the same organization and platform as will be found in the fund. Just because a trader was successful at XYZ Bank – and can prove it – does not mean that he/she will be successful in managing his/her own fund.

☐ How long is the track record?
  ☐ Short (even a year or two) track records may involve a good amount of luck.

☐ How much of the track record is due to the trader or due to other factors such as the seat he/she is sitting in, a good team, good infrastructure, etc.?
  ☐ Team: Will the trader's team be joining him at the new fund?

☐ Will the portfolio of counterparties and associated credit terms be similar to what the trader enjoyed previously?

☐ How quickly will the new fund manager be able to set up an effective organizational infrastructure including mid- and back-office, IT systems, etc.?

☐ What gives the new fund manager her edge?

☐ What is the ideal AUM for a fund manager's particular strategy?

☐ What could go wrong? How likely is this to happen?

☐ What is the greatest risk that would prevent this fund manager from succeeding with this venture?

☐ How volatile is the strategy?

☐ Does the strategy involve an overreliance on leverage for it to be successful?

☐ How liquid is the strategy?

Bibliography

Bern, G. (2011) *Investing in Energy: A Primer on the Economics of the Energy Industry.* John Wiley & Sons: New York.

Edwards, D. (2009) *Energy Trading and Investing: Trading, Risk Management and Structuring Deals in the Energy Market.* McGraw-Hill: New York.

Errera, S. and Brown, S.L. (2002) *Fundamentals of Trading Energy Futures and Options*, 2nd edn. PennWell Books: Tulsa, OK.

Eydeland, A. and Wolyniec, K. (2003) *Energy and Power Risk Management: New Developments in Modeling, Pricing and Hedging.* John Wiley & Sons: Chichester.

Fabozzi, F.J., Füss, R. and Kaiser, D.G. (2008) *The Handbook of Commodity Investing.* John Wiley & Sons: Hoboken, NJ.

Fiorenzani, S., Reavelli, S., and Edoli, E. (2012) *The Handbook of Energy Trading.* John Wiley & Sons: Chichester.

Geman, H. (2005) *Commodities and Commodity Derivatives: Modelling and Pricing for Agriculturals, Metals, and Energy.* John Wiley & Sons: Chichester.

Geman, H. (2009) *Risk Management in Commodity Markets: From Shipping to Agriculturals and Energy.* John Wiley & Sons: Chichester.

Kaminski, V. (2013) *Energy Markets.* Risk Books: London.

Kerr, K. (2005) *Trading Natural Resources in a Volatile Market.* Marketplace Books: New York.

Schenker, J. and Verdon, L. (2012) *Commodity Prices 101.* Prestige Professional Publishing: Austin, TX.

Spurga, R.C. (2006) *Commodity Fundamentals: How to Trade the Precious Metals, Energy, Grain, and Tropical Commodity Markets.* John Wiley & Sons: New York.

PART III

STARTING THE JOURNEY

Chapter 5

The Business Plan: Implications and Applications

The will to win is not as important as the will to prepare to win.
Bob Knight

Introduction

This quote is attributed to Bob Knight, the former basketball coach at the University of Indiana-Bloomington, where he won three NCAA national championships and became equally well known for controversy due to his hot temper and winning ways on the basketball court. In his statement, Knight identifies a critical insight that often separates those who succeed and those who do not. Almost everyone wants to win but most are not willing to sacrifice the time, energy, and effort required to win. This principle is as applicable to starting a successful hedge fund as it is to a championship basketball team.

We feel that drafting a business plan is a critical step required to successfully launch a hedge fund. Until ideas are given structure and words put to paper, the prospect of starting a hedge fund resides squarely in the realm of daydreaming. Writing a business plan forces a potential fund founder to think through critical issues related to investing, risk management, and fund management.

In our experience, the greatest challenge successful traders have when transitioning from an institutional environment such as an investment bank to starting their own funds is the realization that they are no longer solely risk takers but also business owners. They must now think about a whole host of issues that were normally taken care of for them. The business plan serves as a roadmap to guide aspiring fund founders by highlighting decisions that need to be made and by providing milestones that need to be achieved to move the fund from dream to reality.

We discuss many of the substantive topics found in a hedge fund business plan in greater detail throughout this book, however, we feel that having a separate chapter specifically related to business plans is important to help aspiring fund managers as they write their own business plans and to help set up several topics discussed later.

Objectives and Uses of a Hedge Fund Business Plan

A hedge fund business plan consists of unique characteristics that set it apart from business plans one might see used by a technology start-up or a new business selling traditional products. Some of those key differences are highlighted below.

Integrated Business

Almost all hedge funds can be thought of as an integrated business entity that combines, at a minimum, two entities: (1) a fund; and (2) the firm. Essentially, money that is used by a fund for investment activities – as well as the trading positions taken with invested capital – are legally identified to be part of a fund as opposed to the firm.

The firm generally houses the investment manager, or if delegating investment and trading decision, then the investment advisor. Additionally, if appropriate, there may also be investment sub-advisors as appropriate (if delegating to more than one investment advisor). An investment manager can manage more than one fund and is the administrative and management locus of a hedge fund.

Planning Drivers

A hedge fund has unique business requirements that drive the business planning around setting up a hedge fund. Though certainly not exhaustive, some of the key areas that drive business planning are as follows.

- **People requirements.** Although hedge funds can generally start with minimal overheads and a small headcount, the quality and skills of the headcount are absolutely critical since most early-stage hedge funds run very lean. Accordingly, first and foremost, a fund manager needs to ensure that the proper human resources are in place.

- **Infrastructure requirements.** A hedge fund manager must ensure their fund has robust infrastructure in place. This does not necessarily mean being in the nicest office or having the fastest execution speed in the world. What it does mean is ensuring you have access to any technology you need to be successful, which could range from specific software requirements, access to data providers, or any necessary systems to take and manage risk.

- **Service provider requirements.** Since hedge funds generally run lean, they rely on service providers such as accounting firms, administrators, law firms, and prime brokers to provide assistance. The price, quality, and use of service providers will differ according to the size of your fund, your fund's geography, and your fund's trading style. As such, it is worthwhile to think about service providers as early as possible.

- **Financial resources of the founder(s).** Much of a hedge fund's initial capital will likely come from the personal wealth of the fund founder(s). This will continue to be the case until investors have committed capital to the new fund. The fundraising process almost always takes longer than expected. As such, we recommend potential hedge fund managers to ensure they (and if applicable, their dependents) are financially secure enough that a prolonged delay in fundraising will not substantially affect them financially. Lack of sufficient personal financial preparation will take a psychological toll on the new manager and his or her family, leading to greater stress in an already stressful situation, which may ultimately affect investment performance.

- **Market return potential and expectations.** A new fund manager should think about opportunities to generate value and what their expectations are moving forward. Though no one is expecting a new fund manager to predict the future, a hedge fund manager's view of future opportunities and worldview are of great interest to potential investors. When starting a hedge fund, a new manager is implicitly expressing that there is opportunity to make money in the markets moving forward. Explicitly, a new manager should ask themselves: Do I feel I can make money on behalf of my investors? If yes, why do I feel that way? Thinking through these two questions and articulating the 'why' component of the query will be helpful when meeting with potential investors.

- **Risk characteristics.** It goes without saying that the financial industry has seen rough times lately. The experience of the last few years has reminded us of the importance of scenario planning and ensuring risk management practices are well developed. Related to the above, it is also important to craft policy regarding fund drawdowns and think about how to deal with redemptions from investors.

- **Tax.** Tax is a critical driver in the planning, starting, and managing of a hedge fund. A prospective fund manager ignores tax considerations at their peril. Lack of proper tax planning will likely be detrimental to a manager's personal wealth as well as providing an endless source of consternation if not thoroughly explored prior to launching the fund.

AUM Planning

As part of this process, a fund manager must determine the minimum AUM for their fund to launch and to remain active. Minimum AUM will vary depending on trading strategy and will largely be shaped by how much capital a fund manager can initially place into the fund. This is because, for many fund managers, the initial capital for a new hedge fund will almost entirely be coming from their own pocket. There are a few fund managers who are able to launch new funds with significant investment from institutional investors; however, the vast majority of fund managers rely on their own capital and perhaps a small group of friends and acquaintances to get their respective funds off the ground. Even with stellar performance, moving from this initial stage to receiving further injections of capital from larger investors will likely take longer than expected. This should be planned into the fund's business plan.

The process of growing AUM is a key component of any fund's continued success. Thought should be given to how assets will be increased. Additionally, the mindset of the more, the better is not always the case, so target AUM should be defined and a coherent rationale for how and why that target was decided on should be thought through.

Investor Planning and Targeting

With trading strategy in place and an AUM target in mind, a fund manager can then focus on investors. Reaching out to investors, marketing the fund, and maintaining relationships with investors and potential investors requires a dedicated plan by itself. Initially, the fund manager will do much of the planning with inputs from experts – such as prime broker capital introduction teams, consultants, and other service providers. For many funds, as they grow, it may make sense to bring some of this expertise in-house. This will depend on the fund and the types of investor.

As the hedge fund universe is heterogeneous, the investor universe is equally, if not more, heterogeneous. Investors will have different investment timelines, liquidity requirements, desired returns, and other constraints depending on the governance structure by which they operate. For example, a pension fund will be subject to different investment guidelines from a family office. These differences among potential investors must be considered throughout the relationship between a fund and its investors. These differences will manifest themselves in terms of liquidity requirements, length of capital lock-ups, and the process by which capital can be redeemed. Additionally, a fund may negotiate bespoke management and performance fee arrangements with investors on a case-by-case basis.

Feasibility Testing

Though perhaps not a common practice among hedge fund managers, in our experience we find that fund managers who perform feasibility testing can identify areas of strength as well as areas of focus that may require further attention.

Feasibility analysis, a practice frequently used as part of strategic planning, is a systematic analysis of the opportunity, threat, participants, resources, and other variables that go into a significant business decision. A start-up hedge fund, like any new business venture, should assess the feasibility of its business to determine its viability and potential challenges.

This is important for two reasons. First, as a business tool, feasibility testing will highlight areas of concern for a fund manager. Second, investors, service providers, and other parties who will be evaluating the fund will raise many of the issues considered during feasibility testing. As such, we suggest using feasibility testing to get ahead of the curve.

Although there is no patented formula for conducting a feasibility test, successful tests will consider factors such as the market, the risk-taking and risk-management strategy, the firm's intellectual and financial capital, investors, tax considerations, technology, and relationships with service providers.

Beyond the Start

Undoubtedly, a business plan is useful in providing a road map in the early stages of launching a fund. Its usefulness, however, does not end there. We echo the late management guru, Stephen Covey, when he counselled in his best-selling book 7 *Habits of Highly Effective People* to 'begin with the end in mind'. This principle applies equally to hedge funds and their business plans. A business plan should think beyond a fund's launch to its continued successful management. Some key factors worth considering include the following.

1. **Business optimization.** As the fund evolves, much of a manager's time will be spent on what we refer to as 'optimizing the business'. On the risk-taking side, a fund manager will want to identify and maintain an optimal exposure to the market and disciplined guidelines regarding risk and cash management.

There may also be an ideal AUM due to scaling limitations found in energy and commodities markets. For example, in some markets there may be a maximum AUM that can reasonably be deployed without significant impairment to the risk/reward ratio. A fund which exceeds that optimal AUM may find it difficult to efficiently deploy its remaining capital. After spending so much time trying to raise money, wondering what to do with extra money may seem like a nice dilemma but can quickly turn into a nightmare if a fund manager cannot effectively deploy that capital. Thinking through that dilemma at the beginning of the fund will help keep a fund manager disciplined and focused. Part of that process will require evaluating the trade-offs that may exist between deploying more capital in existing markets or extending to new markets. Although final decisions do not have to be made when crafting the business plan, various scenarios should be considered.

Beyond absolute AUM, a manager will want to ensure a proper mix of investors. Not all investor money is good money. If an investor does not understand a fund's investment strategy, this will require a manager to spend additional time and energy educating the investor; time and energy that could have been better used to generate returns. Additionally, investors who do not fully understand a fund's investment strategy or are not fully comfortable with the strategy will frequently be the first to ask for their money back at the slightest hiccup.

2. **Cash management.** It is absolutely critical to have disciplined cash management. Good investors usually do a good job of this when it comes to investing, but managing cash as it relates to dealing with operational expenses is often a different matter. A fund manager can be the best investor in the world, but a hedge fund can still lose money through poor cash management. Avoiding unnecessary waste does not require extraordinary intelligence, just attention to detail.

Cash management begins with understanding cash flow, which will be dictated by fee revenue, divided between management fees and performance fees. It is important to understand what fee structure makes sense for a particular fund and its strategy. Additionally, early investors may insist on some sort of fee discount or other economic incentive. It is important to think through such negotiations carefully as these issues will directly impact cash management. Though 2 and 20 is perceived as some sort of market norm, we have found that this is more perceived convention than actual reality. It is wise to think about what fee structure makes sense in both the short and long run and with which types of investors (e.g., early investors or institutional investors).

Along with rent, the largest regular expense most funds will have is compensation. We assume that fund managers reading this are committed to fair compensation for all their employees. It may be tempting to marginalize junior employees or support staff, but this type of behaviour is often short-sighted since it contributes to low employee morale and high employee turnover. We are not advocating that low performers be rewarded equally well as high performers or everyone from the founder to the secretary be paid equally. What we do advocate is being fair and as transparent as possible.

Beyond fair compensation, compensation scheduling is important as well to manage cash outflows. How frequently will salaries be paid? When will bonuses be paid? What are the implications of those payment schedules in terms of tax planning and the firm's budget?

Part of cash management is also dealing with sustained drawdowns and redemptions. Various drawdown and redemption scenarios should be tested to ensure that the business is sustainable through a drawdown period or in the face of wide-scale redemptions. A fund manager will want to ensure they understand and are comfortable with their drawdown policy.

Early on, a fund manager will need to create discipline around expenses paid to service providers. The expenses for accountants, lawyers, fund administrators, investor relations, new technology, filings, side-letters, etc. have a way of creeping upwards. Yes, it is important to engage quality service providers but it does not require paying top dollar for everything. Clear policies will also need to be established about which entity will pay particular costs. For instance, certain expenses will be covered by the fund with other expenses paid for by the investment manager (or investment advisor as the case may be).

We suggest meeting with various service providers and finding the right balance between cost and service that best fits the needs of your fund and its budget. Additionally, at some juncture there may be a tipping point where it becomes cheaper to bring people in-house instead of outsourcing. A fund manager will not know when that point is unless expenses are actively managed. A fund manager who does not do a good job of managing these expenses early on risks jeopardizing the viability of the firm.

Though potentially tedious initially, making an upfront commitment to planning around these types of expense will make a fund manager's life much easier. Unexpected cash-flow challenges distract fund managers from their primary role as investors. Early discipline and effort will pay long-run dividends by preventing issues from arising down the road.

3. **Evolution.** If a hedge fund launches and becomes a successful ongoing concern, it will undoubtedly face strategic inflection points that should also be considered as part of constructing the fund. These points may not show up in the final business plan but they nonetheless need to be addressed since they will likely appear in various legal documents governing the formation and management of the firm and fund(s).

During the life of the firm, there may be times when it is crucial to value the business. Some examples can include the exit of a founding partner, merger with another fund management company, or the sale of all or part of a fund manager's equity to another fund management company. These are sensitive, critical transition points for the life of any fund and should be given thorough thought before the actual situations arise.

Additionally, as a fund grows it may be necessary to add new advisors or sub-advisors to help invest the fund's capital. If those advisors are a good fit but located in a different geographical area, there will be additional costs related to communication, travel, and infrastructure. Even if not a new geography, success may require expansion in terms of office or staff. Although nothing need be written in stone, these are prospective situations that should also be given some thought.

Reviewing the Plan

It is always a bit embarrassing to reveal one's own work; a little bit of embarrassment now, however, will prevent a lot of misery down the road. Time and again, we have seen very successful traders who have left the convenience of an established institution such as an investment bank and come to the stark realization that they have only minimal understanding of the infrastructure that made their lives so easy. Superior skills as an investor do not automatically equal superior business management acumen, which is why the upfront effort in a good business plan is especially critical for prospective hedge fund managers.

Constructing a business plan will quickly reveal how much a hedge fund manager does not know about starting and running a business. This is okay and expected. A new hedge fund manager should rely on auditors, tax advisors, legal counsel, and other sources of knowledge throughout the life of a fund.

What better time to strengthen those relationships than when the business plan is complete. Although a business plan will likely be crafted with some input from these advisors, a hedge fund manager should absolutely review the business plan with their fund's auditors, accountants, prime broker(s) (e.g., business consulting team or equivalent if available) and lawyers once the plan is finished. The right service providers have likely advised multiple funds and will be able to help you detect omissions, adjust expectations, and further educate you regarding details germane to successfully launching and maintaining a new fund.

Conclusion

Whether you use PowerPoint, word-processing software, or pen and paper we encourage you to commit serious time and thought to creating a thorough business plan. There is no right format. What is key is logical thinking expressed in a clear manner based on valid assumptions and grounded in experience.

To help facilitate business planning, we have included a checklist below. The list is not sacrosanct and should be adjusted based on characteristics unique to the fund manager and the envisioned fund. The list is not intended to be comprehensive but only a possible starting point as you think about drafting a hedge fund business plan. Additionally, please refer to Appendix A for a more granular outline of a sample business plan.

- ☐ Be comprehensive. Information in business plans is frequently used again in other documents such as licence applications and due diligence questionnaires for potential investors in the fund. Putting in the work initially can make your job easier down the road.
- ☐ Set the rules. Be very clear as to how the fund will make money. Discuss the investment approach and process in detail. Also, detail how risk will be managed. What are the fund's risk management guidelines?
- ☐ Include the mundane. What are the potential conflicts of interest and how will they be managed and explained? How will responsibilities be segregated to prevent any compliance breaches? What are the key legal issues? Plan and budget for information technology. Have a business contingency plan.
- ☐ Clients. How will clients be served? At the end of the day, a fund manager is investing capital on behalf of clients. Many times that capital was earned through hard work and sweat and was set aside to provide retirement funds and other benefits for the people we interact with daily, such as our neighbourhood postman, local police officer, and the teachers of our children. As such, client focus should be constant.
- ☐ Culture. A business plan is a great opportunity to outline the culture and principles that not only inform investment style but also shape the type of firm you envision building. We feel that good culture is key in

sustaining long-term success because it assists in creating an environment for good decision-making as well as attracting and retaining the best talent. Culture is also an important part of good governance. Without a culture where good governance is valued, it will be difficult for a start-up hedge fund to grow and mature.

☐ People. A business plan is an opportunity to identify talent gaps. You will not know what type of people you need until you understand where your fund is weak. The greatest investment strategy without the right people supporting and executing those ideas will rarely reach fruition or consistency. Additionally, be sure to hire people who embody the culture that you are trying to create.

Bibliography

McCrary, S.A. (2002) *How to Create & Manage a Hedge Fund.* John Wiley & Sons: Hoboken, NJ. Specifically Chapter 8: Hedge Fund Business Plans.

Chapter 6

Laws, Contracts, and Lawyers

The first thing we do, let's kill all the lawyers.
Dick the Butcher in William Shakespeare's *Henry VI*

Don't Kill Your Lawyer

The well-known line about killing all the lawyers in Shakespeare's *Henry VI* is frequently misinterpreted as support for disdain of lawyers. In fact, however, when taken in the context of *Henry VI*, Shakespeare is actually demonstrating that without lawyers there would be no order and justice.

Shakespeare's nugget of wisdom also applies to starting and running an investment firm. Although you may feel like killing yourself at times, let alone your lawyer, while reviewing various drafts of agreements and contracts, a positive relationship with legal counsel will not only make your efforts in launching and managing an investment firm easier, but getting the proper legal framework in place early will allow for easier management of the firm during the various life events it may experience later.

Based on our own experience, partnering with quality legal counsel is invaluable. Given ever-increasing legal costs, fund founders may be tempted to spend a little less by relying on lawyers who are less experienced and/or established. We have found that any marginal savings to be gained by going cheaper are not worth the loss of expertise, practical advice, and relationships that respected fund lawyers have. Additionally, there is an implicit signalling effect when a fund associates itself with quality service providers that can create intangible value for the fund.

Although we recommend working with good lawyers to guide you through the legal aspects of starting a fund, it is important to have a grasp of the foundational components of the process yourself. This is important because even though your lawyer will give counsel, provide options, and help implement decisions, the fund founder must do the actual decision-making. This chapter highlights the core points a fund founder needs to understand to make those decisions.

In the first part of the chapter, we begin by describing the concept of legal entities relevant to fund management. The chapter then reviews the two components of a hedge fund described earlier in this book: the fund structure (i.e., trading and portfolios) and the firm (i.e., management of the non-portfolio aspects of a hedge fund or investment firm). Starting with the fund structure, we review its components and the important attributes and variations. For each important attribute and variation, we review the contractual documents that define the relationship between the relevant entities. We then do the same for the firm, reviewing its components and the contractual documents that define the relevant relationships among legal entities.

In the second part of the chapter, we review the three main structural design decisions that must be made regarding the legal structure of the fund as well as the firm in general. They are: (1) domicile selection; (2) legal form; and (3) regulatory status selection. To conclude we discuss complex tax structuring, in particular the questions of substance and control, and the tax treatment of fees. The purpose of this part is to make the would-be fund manager or the would-be investor knowledgeable in order to enable him or her to ask the right questions, recognize the important issues, and wisely and efficiently make use of various consulting resources and professional advisors.

Legal Basics for Funds

Concept of Legal Entities

A 'legal entity' is an individual or an organization which is legally permitted to enter into a binding contract, can be sued if it fails to meet its contractual obligations, and, for the purposes of our discussion, is able to hold investments in its own name. 'Legal entity' in our discussion will usually refer to a 'juristic person', which is an artificial entity such as a corporation, a legally established partnership, or a foundation that the law treats for some purposes as if it were a natural person. Thereby the law allows a group of natural persons (and/or other juristic persons) to act as if they were a single composite individual for certain purposes. In some jurisdictions an individual person may, by means of a juristic person, have a separate legal personality other than his own. For purposes of the present discussion, we will rarely deal with 'individual persons' except insofar as an appropriately qualified 'high-net-worth individual' and/or 'experienced investor' may be an investor in a hedge fund in his or her own name.

It is of relevant interest that some 'juristic persons' have a separate legal personality for the purpose of entering into contracts, being sued for failure to perform obligations, and holding investments but, for the purposes of taxation, may be 'invisible'. The choice of a *limited corporation* or a *partnership with limited liability* is significantly driven by the nature and jurisdiction of the investor(s) or shareholder(s). Taxable investors (e.g., high-net-worth individuals or other 'natural persons') in some jurisdictions find it more tax efficient to invest in a *limited partnership*. Such a structure – the *limited partnership* – is generally not taxable in its own right. In accordance with the 'look-through principle', the revenues, expenses, assets, liabilities, gains, and losses of the partnership are allocated on a *pro rata* basis (in accordance with the partnership agreement) to the investors or shareholders(s) where, depending on the tax regime and status of the investor/shareholder, they are often consolidated for tax purposes with the other tax-relevant undertakings of the investor/shareholder. A non-taxable entity (e.g., pension fund), on the contrary, might find a *limited corporation* to be an entirely adequate and sometimes more satisfactory legal entity.

The Two Components of the Hedge Fund Business

The hedge fund business consists of two closely related and cooperating groups of entities that remain legally quite separate.

- **Fund.** In essence, a special form of investment vehicle that undertakes no operative business activity.
- **Firm.** Contains the entities that actually hold the intellectual capital and related infrastructure, whose function it is to develop the investment strategy and execute investment decisions.

Founding investor. Additionally, there is often a third legally separate entity – the founding investor – who may have significant power relative to the fund enterprise.

The Fund

The fund itself is normally established by act of law either as a *limited corporation* or as a *partnership with limited liability*. In the simplest of structures, the fund would consist of one legally established *limited corporation* or *limited liability partnership*. This legal entity may also be referred to as a 'fund vehicle', as the fund is in essence a particular form of 'special purpose vehicle' (SPV). An SPV exists in law to allow the creation of legal entities with a narrowly defined business purpose.

Generally, SPVs are established to allow multiple parties to invest in a common project, asset, or undertaking without the necessity of commingling the assets of the common undertaking with the unrelated assets of the project's manager and/or any of its investors. Furthermore, an SPV is designed such that bankruptcy of one of the investors or the manager does not result in a claim on the assets of the vehicle and, further, bankruptcy of the vehicle itself does not normally give rise to a claim against the manager or an investor. Thus, most SPVs are designed to be bankruptcy remote.

The fund – in essence, an SPV – differs from an operating entity in that the fund itself does not *do* anything. The fund undertakes no *operative* business activity. Instead, it 'holds' or 'owns' the investments that comprise the object of the fund. Investors own the investments through the acquisition of a direct or indirect stake in the fund. It is from profitable redemptions of those stakes, as well as from disbursements of dividends, if any, that investors achieve their return. Normally the fund doesn't have any employees of its own. It doesn't 'contain' or 'include' any capacity for investment decision-making or execution. The fund will:

- hold the investment securities, assets, and related liabilities;
- delegate to an investment manager (or if applicable, an investment advisor) investment decisions on behalf of the fund;
- delegate to service providers, usually via the investment manager (or if applicable, an investment advisor) for the efficient administration of the relationships between the fund's investors and their investments.

Documentation: basic required documents

- Business Registration Certificate
- Articles of Association
- Memorandum of Association
- Regulatory Certification.

Attributes and Variations of the Fund Structure

We will now review important attributes and variations of the standard fund structure.

Founding Shareholder

A quick reading of the offering documents of many funds reveals three different kinds of shareholder: the fund or investment manager, ordinary investors, and a founding shareholder or shareholders. The so-called 'founding shares' often have substantial control but little economic investment value. A founding shareholder usually has, for example, the exclusive right to hire and fire directors of the fund, to modify the articles of association of the fund, to order a voluntary winding up of the fund, and in some cases to create new share classes of the fund.

The purpose of creating a founding shareholder class and assigning these shares to a particular entity or individual is for the fund manager to retain control of operational decisions (such as appointing directors).

Classes of Shares or Partnership Units

Even in the most simply structured funds, there are likely to be different types of investors with different expectations regarding the liquidity of their investment and appropriate fee structures to compensate the fund manager. Even in simple structures, one would expect to find that the shares held by the fund manager carried no fees but a long lock-up or redemption notice period. The shares of an ordinary investor, however, likely include a management fee (e.g., 2% per annum), a performance or incentive fee (e.g., 20% of profits), and redemption constraints such as redemption notices only being permitted on a quarterly basis.

These two different types of investor would normally be reflected in different share classes or different classes of partnership units. The constitutional and offering documents of the fund would recognize different terms and conditions as applying to these two different classes of investment participation (e.g., Class A – ordinary investors, Class B – fund manager shares). The investors in these various share classes hold shares in a commingled portfolio of assets and liabilities. In general, in this simplest of structures, shares held in either of these two classes would rank equally in case of the bankruptcy of the fund or its 'winding up' unless otherwise provided for in the constitutional documents of the fund (e.g., articles of incorporation or partnership agreement) and the offering documents of the fund.

Master–Feeder Fund Structures

The structure of a fund quite often consists of more than one legal entity, with a 'master' and 'feeder' fund approach. Occasionally, the unique requirements associated with different types of investor cannot be adequately met simply through the definition and issuance of different classes of fund shares or partnership units. There are numerous possible structural permutations reflecting the peculiar needs of specific investors. From a legal perspective, a feeder fund is a separate legal entity from the fund. Typically, a feeder fund will be 100% invested in shares of a specific class or classes of shares of the master fund. The feeder fund may not be of the same entity type as the master fund (e.g., limited corporation vs. limited partnership vs. unit trust) and it may not have the same domicile as the master fund (e.g., Delaware, USA vs. Cayman Islands).

The master–feeder fund structure allows the investment manager to manage money collectively for varying types of investor in different investment vehicles without having to allocate trades and while producing the same performance returns for the same strategies. This structure allows for the unified management of multiple pools of assets for investors in different taxable categories.

Feeder funds invest assets in a master fund that has the same investment strategy as the feeder fund. The master fund, often structured as a partnership, generally holds all investment securities, objects, or instruments.[7] The master–feeder structure may include a US limited partnership or limited liability company for US investors and a foreign corporation for foreign investors and US tax-exempt investors. The typical investors in an offshore hedge fund structured as a corporation will be foreign investors, US tax-exempt investors, and offshore funds of funds.

Several examples should suffice to illustrate the types of challenge that may give rise to a master–feeder structure.

(a) *Exchange listing.* Certain types of investor are limited with regard to investing in shares that are not listed on a recognized exchange. Other investors particularly value the additional scrutiny and oversight associated with exchange-listed shares. The fund manager, however, may not want all share classes in the master fund to be subject to exchange rules. Exchange-listed shares usually have much more stringent regulations. For instance, regulations with regard to negotiating 'side letter' terms on fees and liquidity that differ from the offering documents will tend to be more restrictive for exchange-listed shares. As a result, the investment manager may want to create a feeder fund and list its shares on a recognized exchange.

(b) *Regulatory restrictions.* Marketing to certain types of investor in certain jurisdictions may incur regulatory obligations that the fund manager does not want to be applicable to the entire fund. For instance, current US regulations provide that no more than 25% of the assets of a fund may be attributable to Employee Retirement Income Security Act (ERISA)-regulated investors. An administrator especially attuned to the peculiarities of US securities and investment regulations can often best monitor relevant regulatory restrictions. Often a feeder fund designed specifically for different regulatory and tax categories of US investors

---

[7]An exception to this maybe currency hedges for feeder fund shares that are denominated in a currency that is different than that of the master fund.

would be created. Not only must a feeder fund in which US investors invest be ERISA-compliant, but there are often certain additional tax-reporting requirements that must be undertaken by the feeder fund.

(c) *Tax-reporting jurisdictions.* A widely marketed offshore fund might choose to channel all investments from a particular jurisdiction, such as the USA, through one or more feeder funds designed to meet the regulatory requirements of that jurisdiction concerning tax reporting. For example, as mentioned above, US-domiciled investments must be ERISA-compliant. Additionally, funds must provide information for the tax returns of each individual taxable investor in accordance with the rules of the US Internal Revenue Service (IRS). US citizens investing in offshore funds treated as corporations by the IRS, for example, require return information documents as they are subject to tax under the passive foreign investment company (PFIC) provisions of the IRS.[8]

Master–Feeder Fund Structure In Depth

As mentioned above, the structure of a fund quite often consists of more than one entity and is structured using a 'master' and 'feeder' fund approach. There are numerous possible structural permutations reflecting the peculiar needs of specific investors and/or the peculiar needs of specific investments. As a case study, let us consider a structure that is quite often seen in practice and is only moderately complex. It consists of the following entities: the master fund, an 'onshore dollar feeder fund', an 'offshore dollar feeder fund', and an 'offshore euro feeder fund'.

The master fund in our example is incorporated as a 'limited company' in the Cayman Islands and has been registered with the Cayman Islands Monetary Authority (CIMA). It is a trading member of several commodity exchanges, maintains execution brokerage counterparty arrangements with numerous brokers, has several clearing broker bank relationships to clear its transactions through the various exchanges, and maintains direct trading counterparty relationships with several financial institutions and other market counterparties.

The master fund has no employees and no buildings but lots of contracts and a few bank accounts. The master fund has three statutory directors: one appointed from the fund services affiliate of its offshore counsel law firm, one appointed from the master fund's founding investor, and one completely independent director named because of her experience as a director of several other commodity hedge funds. The directors act together to

---

[8]For further information on US requirements, please consult the Internal Revenue Code (PFIC-specific requirements are covered in Sections 1291 through 1298).

oversee the master fund's activities and to guard the interest of investors. Two of the directors are Cayman Islands residents and one is a citizen and resident of another country. The master fund has three separate investment classes (other than that for the founding investor), each with different terms and each class aligned with a specific feeder fund. The master fund is a 'US dollar-denominated fund', meaning that its accounts are maintained in US dollars and its annual reports are prepared in US dollars. Nonetheless, the master fund maintains several bank accounts in different currencies.

The 'onshore dollar feeder fund' is organized as a limited partnership registered in Delaware, only accepts investments from onshore US-domiciled investors, and only accepts US dollars. It is organized as a limited partnership because US tax law makes that the most favourable fund structure for its taxable US investors. Investors acquire limited partnership units in the 'onshore dollar feeder fund'. The 'onshore dollar feeder fund' is 100% invested in the master fund. The 'onshore dollar feeder fund' has one class of investors with regard to the investment terms offered (other than the founding investor). The terms of this single investor class mirror the terms of the relevant investor class in the master fund. The 'onshore dollar feeder fund' has a general partner responsible for its operation. The general partner is a Delaware limited corporation with three directors: a director appointed from the founding investor of the master fund, a director appointed from the corporate services division of the onshore law firm handling the master fund's business vis-à-vis this feeder fund in the USA, and a third director appointed for his knowledge of the fund business sector.

The 'offshore dollar feeder fund' is organized as a limited company registered in the Cayman Islands and only accepts investments from offshore US-dollar investors. These US-dollar investors may in fact include US-domiciled pension funds and other non-taxable entities which do not require the tax benefits associated with the limited partnership structure of the previously discussed 'onshore dollar feeder fund'. The organization of this offshore feeder mirrors that of the onshore dollar feeder fund, and so it is also organized as a limited partnership. Investors acquire limited partnership units in the feeder fund that are 100% invested in the master fund. The terms of this single investor class mirror the terms of the relevant investor class in the master fund, and so on. However, the 'offshore dollar feeder fund' is aimed at offshore investors, and has the same three directors as the master fund.

The 'offshore euro feeder fund' is organized as a limited company registered in the Cayman Islands. It only accepts euro-denominated investments that are offshore to Europe. Again, it has the exact same three directors as the master fund, and the same single share class concept.

Each of these feeder funds and the master fund require a number of operational oversight processes: 'administration' by an administrator, an auditor,

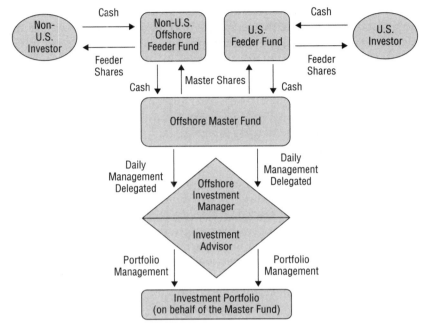

FIGURE 6.1 Master–feeder diagram.
Source: Stable Asset Management.

etc. They also require regulatory registration in the Cayman Islands, except the 'onshore dollar feeder fund' which requires US registration.

Figure 6.1 visually lays out much of the structure discussed thus far in the chapter. Although not an exact replica of the case study immediately above, this figure gives a general sense of the relationship between the different legal entities.

Control Agreement for Master–Feeder Funds

Sometimes, in master–feeder fund structures, the relationship between the two entities will be defined by a 'Control Agreement for Master–Feeder Funds'.

Side-Pocket Structures

Thus far our discussion of the fund structure has been limited to legal and regulatory facts that are primarily focused on the peculiarities of investors of different types, domiciles, and tax statuses. The fund structure, whether a simple standalone fund with various share classes or a master–feeder fund structure, defines the nature of the investment assets from the point of view of the investor. There are, however, other legal peculiarities of fund structures that have more to do with the specific strategies traded and the organization of the activities of the investment manager and its investment advisor and investment sub-advisor.

When all of the assets held by the fund's portfolio are traded in transparent and liquid markets such as some of the larger energy exchanges, it is likely that – from the legal and accounting perspective – all of the assets are commingled and held in the name of the single fund or master fund. Occasionally, however – either intentionally or as a result of changing market conditions – the fund will find that it owns investment assets that are infrequently traded, illiquid, or traded in markets lacking transparency and will find it difficult or impossible to value those assets for a significant period of time. Nonetheless, the portfolio manager may expect that the likely potential future value of the asset is significant enough to warrant holding those assets in the fund over a long period of time. It may be impossible to value the assets for many months until a certain future liquidity event. In general practice, such an asset is 'ring-fenced' or assigned to a 'side-pocket'.

A new class of shares would normally be created exclusively to hold the investment in the side-pocket. Existing shareholders would redeem enough shares on a pro-rata basis to buy all of the shares in the new share class associated with the investment held ring-fenced in the side-pocket. These new side-pocket shares would normally have very specific terms describing the liquidity event (or events) that would lead to a valuation of the shares and the subsequent assessment of fees. At this point, investors could potentially redeem the shares held in the side-pocket. Normally neither management fees nor performance fees would be assessed and paid prior to the liquidity event, given that assessment of fees normally presumes the ability to value the assets. Unless the assets are to be valued based on original cost, the inability to value the assets is precisely the reason they were assigned to the side-pocket to begin with.

There are several important implications of creating a side-pocket. New investors in the fund purchase shares of the fund portfolio excluding the assets assigned to the side-pocket. Investors who were shareholders at the time assets were assigned to the side-pocket may have the right to redeem shares in the remainder of the fund; however, the redemption terms applicable to shares they hold in the share class associated with the side-pocket are likely to be much more restrictive.

A more serious matter is the legal segregation of the assets and liabilities of the side-pocket from the assets and liabilities of the remainder of the fund.

If there is no formal process of legal segregation, and either the side-pocket or the fund portfolio became insolvent, the insolvent portion of the portfolio would normally have a claim on the assets of the legally undifferentiated solvent portion of the portfolio. This could lead to claims against the fund as well as its portfolio manager from investors in the share classes that owned the solvent portion of the portfolio. Thus, legal segregation is important.

The two most commonly used approaches to eliminate this cross-liability challenge are ring-fencing through contractual agreements and the creation of 'segregated portfolio companies'. The first approach requires that each investor in the fund enters into a limited recourse agreement (i.e., a contract to limit their claims) with the fund. This means the investor acknowledging that they only have claim to the assets of the particular 'side-pocket' and no claim against any other assets of the fund. In most jurisdictions this contractual ring-fencing is widely used and has stood the test of insolvency cases, the exception being claims from non-contractual parties (such as tax claims from tax authorities such as the UK Inland Revenue).

The second approach is not contractual but statutory, which means it is not established through contract but according to existing laws. Creating 'segregated portfolio companies' is essentially to divide the fund into separate, statutorily defined 'segregated portfolios' (sometimes called 'cells'). The statutory ring-fencing separates the assets to ensure there are no cross-portfolio claims. It is worth noting, however, that if insolvency is managed in a jurisdiction that does not recognize the laws on which the statutory segregation is based, then this method may not be effective.

To avoid the limitations of each approach, both approaches are sometimes used simultaneously to ensure no cross-liability risks exist between different portfolios within the fund. An example of illiquid assets that might be candidates for a 'sub-fund', 'side-pocket', or 'segregated portfolio company' treatment includes speculative and hard-to-value investments. Such assets would typically be found if a fund were investing in logistics assets such as transmission, transportation, or storage capacity. In circumstances where these capacities or assets are purchased in advance of their intended use and in the absence of active futures or forward markets for them, it may be necessary to wait months or years before actually realizing the value of investing in them.

While such investments may prove to be particularly valuable, they may be nearly impossible to value objectively until months or years after their acquisition. During this long period, the ownership of the commingled portfolio may change significantly. It therefore becomes an issue of fairness to ensure that the investors at the time of the acquisition of these assets remain exposed, in undiluted ratios, to the risks and potential returns of the investment. Additionally, this segregation can make borrowings in support of such an acquisition more feasible. A creditor may often feel more comfortable loaning money for an asset-based investment such as logistics capacity, while feeling quite uncomfortable being exposed to the overall risk of the fund portfolio.

The Firm

An investment firm consists of the entities that actually contain the intellectual capital and related infrastructure, whose function it is to develop the investment strategy, make investment decisions, execute those decisions, monitor risks associated with those investment decisions, etc. Even though the firm can outsource some of these activities, the firm is ultimately responsible for providing the essential investment-related intellectual capital. The following are the core entities that comprise an investment firm:

- **Investment manager.** Responsible for managing the processes and activities necessary to enable the execution of the fund investment strategy. In some documents, the Investment Manager may be referred to as the Manager, and the Investment Advisor as the Investment Manager, this is especially prevalent in the United Kingdom when structures have onshore investment teams.
- **Investment advisor.** Responsible for the tactical execution of the investment strategy.
- **Investment sub-advisor.** Responsible for the execution of a particularly defined part of the investment strategy assigned (usually a single trader or small team of traders). An Investment Sub-Advisor may not always be necessary.

It is important to note that the existence and domicile of the investment manager, investment advisor, and any investment sub-advisor are driven by the realities of the intellectual capital that determines the investment strategy and their organizational infrastructure: who the investment managers are, who the traders are, where they work, and what tools they need to work with (computers, models, communications, IT, etc.).

The type of legal entity the investment manager, investment advisor, and any investment sub-advisor takes (such as limited company vs. limited partnership), and the nature of the contractual relationships they have to service providers, is driven by non-investment strategy-related aspects such as: investor marketing, liability shielding, tax structuring, regulatory compliance, and regime selection.

Investment Manager

The investment manager is the entity responsible for managing the processes and activities necessary to execute the fund investment strategy. It is the overarching entity that coordinates, organizes, and directs investment strategy.

The investment manager will often be organized as a limited partnership in the same domicile as the fund. A limited company is usually created to act as general partner. This limited company acting as general partner normally has one or more offshore independent directors. In addition, it may also have a director who, though not offshore, is either drawn from among the ranks of the team that founded the fund or is a well-trusted and close advisor. This investment manager, 'Investment Manager LP' and its general partner, 'Investment Manager Ltd' normally do not contain the intellectual capacity and related infrastructure to develop investment strategy, make investment decisions, etc.

In general, the investment manager and the entities that comprise it are established for tax efficiency, liability, and regulatory purposes. Nevertheless, they do perform an important management function by managing the processes and activities of the fund structure and the firm. Without this management the fund would not be able to function. Many would-be fund managers see the investment manager from purely a tax-efficiency and liability-shielding point of view. This is unwise. Most, if not all, tax authorities will quickly realize if an investment manager is not performing the roles it should be, and what kind of approach to the hedge fund business that fund employs: a fraudulent one.

The set of rules the US IRS uses to determine whether or not certain foreign funds are a US business is known as 'The Ten Commandments'. This set of rules is used to determine which activities the investment manager must perform offshore if the fund wishes to be considered as under offshore jurisdiction. They include activities such as communication with shareholders and the general public, maintaining and auditing the books, or holding director and shareholder meetings. For the investment manager structure to be tax efficient by performing activities offshore, it is obvious that it must perform said activities offshore.

Investment Management Agreement

The fund delegates the responsibility for organizing and managing the processes that enable the execution of investment strategy decisions to the investment manager through the investment management agreement between the fund and the investment manager. The directors of the fund will, for liability reasons, be eager to demonstrate that they have delegated responsibility to the firm, however, this delegation of responsibility to the firm has tax and liability consequences. The investment manager will also be documented through the:

- Registration Certificate
- Articles of Association
- Regulatory Certification (specific for each jurisdiction).

Investment Advisor

The investment advisor is a legal entity contracted to the investment manager to execute the investment strategy. Normally, the investment manager has delegated most or all investment decisions to the investment advisor. The investment advisor entity is normally domiciled in the same legal jurisdiction where the actual intellectual capital behind the fund is located and works on a day-to-day basis. The decision whether to establish the investment advisor as a limited company or a limited partnership (requiring a general partner) is primarily driven by tax concerns and the law of the respective jurisdiction.

The investment advisor can subcontract some (or all) of the investment activities to one or more investment sub-advisors. We discuss the investment sub-advisors below.

The Investment Advisory Agreement

An investment advisory agreement is contracted between the investment manager and the investment advisor. The investment advisor will also have the:

- Registration Certificate
- Articles of Association
- Regulatory Certification (specific for each jurisdiction).

Investment Sub-Advisor

The investment sub-advisor is a legal entity designed to hold additional intellectual capital dedicated to the purpose of defining investment strategy. The investment advisor can subcontract some (or all) of the investment activities to one or more investment sub-advisor. This is often a structure used when there are actually several different discrete teams (with, perhaps, clearly identifiable trading responsibilities) or when discrete teams have different locations and local managements (and perhaps compensation structures).

The Investment Sub-Advisory Agreements

The investment sub-advisory agreement is contracted between the investment advisor and one or more investment sub-advisors. The investment sub-advisor will also have the:

- Registration Certificate
- Articles of Association
- Regulatory Certification (by region).

Attributes and Variations of the Investment Management Enterprise

We will now review important attributes and variations of the standard investment management enterprise structure.

Governance Processes

Several governance processes might be used in the structuring of an investment firm. Governance processes are related to the activities to be performed within the firm, particularly those pertaining to the investment manager. Processes like regular board meetings with detailed minutes, regular strategy meetings with detailed minutes, compliance and performance meetings, etc. form a crucial part of the practical steps which need to be taken to ensure a robust governance structure for the firm and, by implication, for the fund.

Considerations on Contractual Documentation

Having reviewed the contractual documentation, there are some general considerations that are helpful to keep in mind while reviewing each of the contracts involved in setting up the fund structure and the firm structure. They are generic considerations that underline the most important aspects affected by the nature and terms of each contractual relationship. Each of the aforementioned contractual documents must be evaluated with the following aspects in mind.

- Marketing: the nature of the contractual relationships will be important from a marketing perspective vis-à-vis not only investors but also service providers and other stakeholders as well. Each party will have preferences around who retains control for what functions, where each entity is domiciled, etc.
- Liability transfers/retentions/indemnifications: the actual principals of the fund management business are likely to be interested in having as many layers of liability blockers as possible between them and their personal assets. On the contrary, service providers and directors are unlikely

to want to 'wear' any risk for trading, risk management, and regulatory decisions they did not make.

- Tax implications (especially related to control issues).
- Consistency with the offering documents and the articles of association of the various entities involved.
- Consistency with the regulatory status of the contracting entities.

Structural Design Decisions

We now review the three main structural design decisions that must usually be made regarding the legal structure of the fund as well as the firm in general. They are domicile selection, legal form selection, and regulatory status selection. To conclude, we discuss complex tax structuring, in particular the questions of substance and control, and the tax treatment of fees.

In general, there are three important decisions that must usually be made regarding the legal structure of the fund structure and the firm structure:

1. Domicile selection
2. Legal form selection
3. Regulatory status selection.

These decisions are driven by three characteristics of the fund. (1) What is the investment strategy? (2) Where is the location from which investment strategy decisions will be made? In other words, into what commodities, through what instruments, through what platforms, and in what markets does the fund wish to invest, and where will the intellectual trading capital be located? (3) To a lesser degree, what type of investors will be targeted, and what are their nationalities and location of domicile?

The decision drivers associated with structural design decisions can be quite complex and often conflicting in practice. Optimizing among the various possible design combinations will be one of the most time-consuming and critical activities during the business planning phase. It is an exercise of trade-offs. This process is, of course, not entirely irreversible since it is often possible to restructure both the fund structure and the firm following launch. Post-launch restructuring, however, has considerable downsides:

- it is usually much more expensive than taking the time to get it right the first time;
- it often has tax consequences because it creates a taxable event;

- it often requires the consent of investors, which gives the investors an opportunity and leverage to negotiate other unrelated matters.

Post-launch restructuring is incredibly time-consuming and tedious. It's like repairing a complex piece of moving machinery while it is operating, as opposed to building the machine correctly before operation begins. Virtually every counterparty of an entity being restructured must be involved in the restructuring process. This means director signatures, notarizations, apostilles, reruns of compliance and operational due diligence, etc.

A fund manager can expect to be involved with a variety of consultants during the structural design process: tax advisors, legal advisors, regulatory advisors, representatives of intended investors, and service providers. During this time it will become clear that not all investors and not all individuals involved in the firm necessarily have the same tax or regulatory interests. If a hedge fund includes traders or advisors in more than one country or state, it should not be surprising if they have very different needs with respect to tax structure. One should not rush this process; it will be iterative and take some time. The key objective should be to identify the necessary considerations and ensure that the original structural design process is adequately comprehensive with regard to the matters that it considers and addresses.

A hedge fund manager would be wrong to conclude that the matter is so complex that it is best left entirely to an international securities and tax law firm as selected by a prime broker. Many of the international firms subcontract – either out of necessity or convenience – portions of their work to local firms in offshore or other national jurisdictions. The layering of fees with bankers supervising lawyers supervising more lawyers and audit firms and tax advisors is a guaranteed way to spend a lot of money fast and to create an enduringly complex and expensive structure. A good legal structure for a hedge fund enterprise should not be delegated to lawyers and advisors, just like one should not delegate the legal structure for a complex commodity transaction.

The purpose of this section is to make the would-be fund manager or the would-be investor knowledgeable in order to enable him or her to ask the right questions, recognize important issues, and wisely and efficiently make use of various consulting resources and professional advisors.

The domicile selection, legal form selection, and regulatory status selection decisions will be treated as if they were a sequential process. Furthermore, these matters shall be treated as if the fund structure and the firm structure can be considered separately or in isolation. In reality, however, both decisions must be made simultaneously for both the fund structure and the firm structure. Like most complex business structuring decisions, it will be an optimization process with multiple variables to be traded off against each other.

Domicile Selection

When we speak of domicile in this section, we refer to legal domicile. A corporation or a partnership has a legal domicile within a specific legal jurisdiction and is subject to the laws of that jurisdiction. In most cases, the jurisdiction has a public agency that is responsible for registering corporations and partnerships as well as handling the administrative law aspects governing their creation, existence, modification, termination, sale, transfer, and insolvency.

Legal domiciles tend to be very specific because the governing laws and administering agencies tend to be very geographically specific. It would not be enough, for instance, to say that a legal entity is domiciled in the USA or in Switzerland. It is also necessary to identify the state or canton, as the case may be to know the correct legal domicile. There is, for instance, within the USA considerable difference from state to state in terms of corporate law. While the differences are not as great among the cantons of Switzerland as the states of the United States, they are still relevant.

Legal domicile is not automatically the same as tax domicile or 'residence'. While it is virtually automatic that, for instance, the Cayman Islands would consider a Cayman Islands legally domiciled fund to also be tax domiciled in the Cayman Islands (and thus not subject to any tax), it would be relatively easy through poor structural planning for the Swiss tax authorities or the US tax authorities to determine that the Cayman Islands legally domiciled fund was a Swiss or US fund for purposes of taxation.

This imputed tax distinction falls under various tax doctrines including, for instance, that of 'permanent presence'. Once again, when we refer to domicile in this section, we refer to the legal jurisdiction that has registered the fund. We are not referring to 'choice of laws'.

For example, in the contracts prescribing the delivery of services between two Cayman Islands entities, the contracting counterparties occasionally agree that the contract will be interpreted and governed under the laws of, for instance, the State of New York. Occasionally, even a non-Cayman Island jurisdiction will be chosen for settling of disputes – such as by arbitration. Once again, this is a separate matter from the legal domicile of a legal entity. This 'choice of laws' or 'jurisdiction for settlement of disputes' is an important legal matter but is beyond the scope of this book and, in any case, is not essential material to be mastered by hedge fund managers or investors.

The following are the principal drivers that substantially impact domicile selection.

Regulatory Environment and Framework

- **Stability and predictability.** Is the regulatory system and its related institutions widely understood and stable? All hedge fund-related regulation

is constantly under review but it is important for investors and investment managers alike to be able to trust that the general system which
they are adopting is relatively predictable, transparent, consistently
enforced, and not subject to 'behind the scenes' influence on the part
of counterparties or interests groups which could be detrimental to the
investor or the fund manager.

- **Degree of regulation, the balance of 'loose' and 'tight'.** Investors and fund
  managers will want a system that they can trust as being fair and consistently applied. They will, however, not want an exhaustive (and exhausting)
  system of regulation that leads to substantial investment of time, substantial legal and regulatory compliance costs, and a substantial potential for
  accidentally violating a regulation with resulting serious consequences.
- **Pivotal industry player power.** Which interests are the principal drivers of
  change in the regulatory regime and which interested parties are routinely
  involved and consulted prior to changing the regulatory system? In some
  jurisdictions, such as Germany, the pressure for change in the regulation
  of hedge funds seems to come primarily from political forces that are not
  typically friendly to the deployment of any form of speculative capital or
  the earning of money from speculative market behaviour. Fund managers and investors are occasionally included in discussions about regulatory strategy, but do not appear to be either the driving or a significant
  mitigating force in determining final decisions on regulation. In a fluid
  regulatory environment one could reasonably predict that the regime will
  change in ways unfriendly to both fund managers and investors.
- **National bias.** The variety of regulation available to a hedge fund often
  depends on whether investors will be local or foreign. Most offshore
  domiciles have very different regulations for funds that allow local individuals to invest. As long as investors are foreign individuals or firms, a
  more friendly regulation regime tends to be available.
- **Applicability of law.** As mentioned above with regard to taxes, there are
  many ways that a fund or fund manager domiciled in one jurisdiction
  can accidentally be interpreted by a regulator in another jurisdiction to
  be subject to the regulations of that jurisdiction they are not domiciled
  in. In the USA, Switzerland, and even the UK, failure to pay careful attention to the local regulations – especially as concerns the marketing of the
  fund to investors and the acceptance of investments – can result in being
  accidentally interpreted as being subject to that local regulatory regime
  (along with its rules, registration, and reporting requirements).

Taxes

- **Degree of tax neutrality.** In most cases, the ideal domicile for a hedge fund
  entity is one that is 'tax neutral'. In other words, the tax implications of

the investment should be primarily driven by the tax positions of the investors themselves rather than by the domicile of the fund. The Cayman Islands, for instance, along with most other offshore domiciles, ensure 'tax-free operations' for investment vehicles that are essentially handling offshore business (rather than local Cayman Islands activities). The Cayman Islands even goes as far as to provide a government certification ensuring that any change in tax law that would result in the fund or fund manager being liable to taxation would not be applied for 20 years – essentially ensuring permanent non-taxable status.

- **Hidden taxes.** It is important to look for 'hidden taxes'. Besides taxes on the profits of the fund or on dividends – both types of tax that are frequently non-existent in offshore domiciles – it is important to look for various types of so-called 'stamp taxes'. Even in most 'tax-efficient' regimes such as the Cayman Islands and Switzerland, there can be taxes or tax-like fees on such transactions as authorization of new shares in the fund or the firm. In the case of Switzerland, for example, a stamp tax is due on certain types of investment transaction.

- **Trade-off in tax interests between investors and the investment management enterprise.** Domicile issues must always be considered when balancing the tax interests of the investors and the firm. There are domicile combinations that do not work well together. For example, it may be the case that for a certain fund it is easier to structure a fund with a Cayman Islands domicile for US investors and a fund with Guernsey or Luxembourg domicile for EU investors.

- **Trade-off in tax interests between the firm and the fund.** It is often easier to consider the tax implications of the domicile of the fund rather than the implications of the domicile of the firm. If the fund is offshore, it is unlikely that the actual intellectual capital activity of the firm will physically take place on the soil of the legal territory of that domicile. For example, an investment manager that is physically located in London, New York, Zurich, or Frankfurt will have a difficult time claiming, for instance, that it should be considered Cayman Islands resident for tax purposes. All tax authorities, almost without exception, will look to determine where the 'control' lies. Control lies wherever the actual individuals making the decisions are resident. Tax authorities will suspect that an investment manager located in the Cayman Islands or other offshore regime is a 'shell company' with no 'tax substance'. This is particularly true when there is no effective tax treaty between the regime that is the domicile of the investment manager and the jurisdiction in which the intellectual capital is actually located and working.

Many of the legal entities, including, for instance, the 'founding investor' attempt to solve challenges posed by competing tax regimes and their sensitivities. The area concerning the taxation of an investment manager's other firm components and individual fund managers is currently fluid. Even very stable tax and regulatory jurisdictions such as the UK are paying careful attention to the taxability of offshore revenues and attributable capital gains. Later in this chapter we discuss some of the tools of tax structuring which are often employed to address tax-related challenges.

Customer Friendliness

- **Administrative complexity.** How easy and expensive is it to deal with the various administrative agencies in the candidate domicile? What hidden costs are there, such as excessive local counsel or notarial actions associated with transactions with the administrative agencies? The most efficient offshore domiciles have extensively automated the standard processes of registering a new company or partnership, changing its name, recording its incumbent directors, filing its regulatory documents, etc. In regimes of high customer friendliness, local law firms may be connected directly via computer to the required agencies with the result that companies and partnerships can be created and registered almost in real time, offering memoranda can be filed automatically and immediately, fees nearly instantly transferred, etc. Key questions helpful to determine administrative complexity include: How quickly and inexpensively may an entity be created, renamed, or changed? How quickly and inexpensively can its articles of association or incorporation or other governance documents be changed? How quickly and inexpensively may directors be legally appointed and/or removed? How quickly and inexpensively may required regulatory documents be filed? How time-consuming will it be to complete the regulatory documents?
- **Ease and cost of maintenance.** In addition to the complexity and cost involved in certain actions, one must also consider how complex and costly the ongoing maintenance of the structure is after set-up. For example, what are the requirements and costs of annual registration? What are the requirements for annual shareholders and periodic directors' meetings? What are the requirements for filing of audited or unaudited annual reports? What are the costs, speed, and ease of obtaining frequently required documents such as official lists of directors as recorded with the corporate registry, certificates of good standing, certified copies of articles or certificates of incorporation, etc.?

Case Study: Customer Friendliness

In the Cayman Islands, a complete firm structure could easily be registered, populated by legally appointed directors, and approved for required regulatory filings and exemptions within one week. That includes signing the investment management agreement and other contracts among the newly created entities. This assumes, of course, that the investment manager already has a relationship with local counsel and that the local counsel already maintains anti-money-laundering and 'know your customer' (KYC) compliance documentation on the relevant parties including the investment manager and the founding investor (if there is to be one). The Cayman Islands work diligently to ensure that they are the most efficient place in the world to domicile a hedge fund. There are of course some challenges, such as the time difference, that need to be considered.

Brand

*   **Domicile brand.** Countries have brands. For example, countries like Macau and Cyprus undoubtedly offer tax advantages and easy regulatory environments for a fund. Many international investors, however, would feel uncomfortable investing in a fund that was domiciled in Macau or Cyprus. Their instinctive discomfort is associated with the brand of that domicile. The brand of Cyprus as a domicile, whether justly or unjustly, is often associated with money laundering, non-transparent activities, and even criminal activities. At the opposite end of the spectrum, places like Jersey or the Cayman Islands work hard to defend their reputable brand as a domicile for funds.

    Therefore, it is crucial to know what brand value each potential domicile has in the eyes of the target investors of a fund. If investors trust the particular regulatory and legal regime of a domicile, they will feel more comfortable with the fund being domiciled there. They will see integrity, transparency, and fairness in brands they trust. Additionally, they will be more familiar with the domicile characteristics, such as their tax regime. Not only do the investors have an interest in the domicile and its reputation or brand. Many service providers are particularly concerned with the integrity and the quality of anti-money-laundering, KYC, and other anti-fraud measures. Last, but not least, fund managers must also realize that a domicile brand will be a proxy for its regulatory and legal dependability.

    Offshore, tax-neutral domiciles have to work constantly in order to maintain and defend their brands. A handful of high-profile cases of tax fraud or laundering of tainted money can do a great deal of damage to the brand of a jurisdiction. As a result of the increasing competition between jurisdictions to attract more hedge fund and other investment fund clients, many of the offshore jurisdictions have greatly tightened their due diligence and KYC requirements. Of course, any jurisdiction that is tax neutral is wide open to tax abuse and avoidance. Many of these offshore jurisdictions are increasingly tightening their regulations to ensure that business undertakings have real business substance rather than only the avoidance of taxes. As a consequence, managers setting up offshore funds will often find that honest and respected directors become nervous or uncomfortable around too much emphasis on tax efficiency.

Availability of Knowledgeable Service Providers

- **Local bias.** Many jurisdictions insist on requiring that certain types of service provider be locally approved. They include:
  o Registered office services
  o Directors
  o Administrators
  o Auditors.

    Not only do these measures help them protect their brand against the presence of substandard service providers, they also ensure that a thriving local industry is created within the boundaries of the jurisdiction.

- **Service provider regulation.** Strict requirements concerning the regulation of service providers are a sign of jurisdiction stability and dependability. Rarely will a fund manager or investor actually physically visit the offshore jurisdiction with any regularity. For this reason, service provider regulation ensures the availability of highly qualified service providers. Some respected jurisdictions will permit non-local administration or audits but require a locally licensed service provider to be officially responsible for providing the service.

Legal Environment

Public Listing Requirements

- **Public listing motivations.** There are a variety of reasons why a fund would consider public listing. Rarely is it to facilitate true liquid public trading of the shares of the hedge fund. More commonly it is motivated by the following reasons:
  o To allow investments by entities that are restricted to investing only in listed securities.
  o To give certain investors the comfort of believing that the listing exchange or agency provides an additional level of regulatory oversight which helps ensure the fair and transparent treatment of the investor.
  o Tax structuring.

- **Domicile vs. public listing jurisdiction.** It is not necessarily required that a fund be domiciled in the same jurisdiction in which it is listed or vice versa. For instance, there is no reason why a Cayman Islands-domiciled fund cannot be listed on the Channel Islands Stock Exchange or the Dublin Stock Exchange. If it is envisioned that a listing may be required at a future point in time, it is important that a fund ensures the likely listing exchanges would be willing to recognize a fund domiciled in an otherwise proposed jurisdiction. In general, a well-regulated, transparent, and fair domicile jurisdiction with a good reputation is likely to be acceptable as the domicile of a fund to be listed on major exchanges.
- **Exchange characteristics.** Fund managers must review the characteristics of available exchanges from a legal point of view since not all exchanges are 'approved' or 'recognized exchanges'. Additionally, it is not always necessary for a listing to be on a 'recognized exchange'. It is important to review the level and source of 'recognition' that an exchange has before determining that it is indeed sufficiently and appropriately 'recognized'. Additionally, some exchanges will only list legal entities incorporated in their own jurisdiction. Others will only list corporations and not limited partnerships.
- **Speed, cost, and complexity of listing.** The speed, cost, and complexity of listing vary dramatically from exchange to exchange. The Caymans Stock Exchange and Channel Islands Stock Exchange claim to be able to manage a listing within three to six weeks of application, assuming all is in order. Practically speaking, it is reasonable to expect the entire process to take under eight weeks. Dublin, for example, is more likely to take six months or more. AIM, a sub-market of the London Stock Exchange, and some other exchanges can be considerably more time-consuming and complex.
  - Listing fees can be considerable, including those for a local jurisdiction 'sponsor'. These should be carefully compared.
  - A listing in the same jurisdiction as the normal offshore counsel and service providers is likely to increase speed and reduce cost by reducing the number of layers of service providers (e.g., Cayman Islands counsel and Guernsey counsel, Cayman Islands auditors and Guernsey auditors).

Legal Form Selection

The second structural design decision is that of the legal form of the fund and its firm. It is worth emphasizing that the legal structures that compose a hedge fund business collectively include elements of corporate law, contract law, and securities law. For instance, a fund will prepare an Information Memorandum, which is substantially a securities law compliance document complete with warnings and restrictions but also has many characteristics of contract law. In it, the fund – and by implication the firm as its contracted service provider – commits to certain guidelines such as the investment restrictions and risk parameters. Intentional violations of those commitments can have implications in securities law but can also lead to liabilities for breach of the contractual terms that govern investments. Legal form is therefore also of critical importance, and relevant in terms of the legal system as a whole, not only securities law. This may cover aspects such as the role of arbitration in courts or the role of common vs. case law with respect to disputes.

- **Stability and transparency.** Hedge fund-related law is constantly evolving. In certain jurisdictions, however, there is already a very well-developed body of law and regulatory policy. Professional investment associations such as the Alternative Investment Management Association (AIMA), as well as local service providers, can share insights into how the local law has evolved and will continue to evolve relative to hedge funds. It is crucial to be convinced of the future stability and transparency of the legal environment of a jurisdiction.
- **Legal friendliness to hedge funds.** Some jurisdictions intentionally attempt to attract hedge fund businesses. They compete with other jurisdictions to have the most developed legal framework, the best customer service-oriented administrative offices, etc. Some time spent on the phone talking with potential offshore counsel and other service providers will give you a fairly good impression as to whether the institutions of the jurisdiction – more than just its laws and agencies – are culturally friendly to the fund management business.
- **Legal system: UK common law vs. continental civil law.** Nearly every place on the globe that was once ruled by Great Britain continues to operate under a UK common law regime (including the USA (except Louisiana), Cayman Islands, British Virgin Islands, Singapore, Bahamas, etc.). Those operating with legal systems based on British common law traditions have the advantage that many lawyers throughout the world – not only in that jurisdiction – will feel comfortable understanding contracts and other legal structures designed for that jurisdiction. There is a vast difference in the structure and assumptions behind continental civil law as opposed to a common law environment. Most hedge funds in the world, as well as their fund managers, are domiciled in common law jurisdictions.

Ease of Structure Change

- **Cooperation with structures in other jurisdictions.** If the fund is successful, it will inevitably be necessary to evolve the structure of the fund and its related entities. If the primary domicile of the fund is widely respected and accepted, it is more likely possible to add new related structures (e.g., segregated funds or feeder funds) without the original domicile becoming a fatal flaw of the structure.

Regulatory Status Selection

The third structural design decision is that of the regulatory status of the fund and its firm. Regulation in different jurisdictions tends to be focused on one or more of the following:

- The fund itself – its transparency, trading, what it trades in, how it is valued, etc.
- The marketing process – to whom the fund can be marketed, by whom, where, and how?
- The investing process – who does the investing or trading. Do they have adequate experience? Do they understand ethical principles regarding 'late trading', 'market manipulation', and other issues necessary to maintain high ethical standards? Do they understand and employ risk-management processes? Do they have the infrastructure necessary for the investment activities anticipated by the fund and do they have enough capital to survive while trading the fund?

Often, the fund itself and the parties responsible for marketing can escape regulations merely based on the type of entities to which they market the fund (e.g., very high-net-worth experienced investors, professional investment groups, corporate treasuries, etc.). Not all jurisdictions require that the firm and/or investment advisor and/or investment sub-advisor be regulated. Different commodity trading platforms in different jurisdictions may have different rules in this regard.

Case Study: Complex Tax Structuring

We conclude this chapter with a case study-type discussion on complex tax structuring, to illustrate the tax considerations implicit in legal entity design for a hedge fund business. We cover the particular tax questions of substance and control as well as the tax treatment of fees.

Tax Structuring: The Example Fund

To more easily tackle the question of complex tax structuring, we shall discuss the tax-optimal structure for a fund of the following characteristics.

- Domiciled in the Cayman Islands.
- Most investors are fund-of-funds and family offices based in Europe.

- Some US investors.
- Investment manager: desire to establish in Cayman Islands for tax purposes.
- Investment advisor: services including some trading in Switzerland.
- Investment sub-advisor: trading activities within the EU, such as London.

Substance and Control

The challenge of the investment manager is that it is essentially a shell company in its chosen jurisdiction (in this example, the Cayman Islands). When tax authorities assess the tax liability of a fund structure and its corresponding firm structure, they look to two key factors: substance and control.

Substance

The investment manager is eager to demonstrate that it actually has significant substance in the Cayman Islands. Substance is taken to mean that real, substantive things happen there, that key decisions are made there. Increasingly, tax authorities look for evidence such as employment agreements and office rental agreements. Furthermore, authorities will expect an address, telephone number, and e-mail address which are not at the offshore counsel office or some other registered office services company. A PO Box address c/o a law office with a telephone number answered by the registered office division of a law office is most persuasive *against* there being any real substance in the offshore domicile.

A common effort to resolve this will be for the Swiss and EU-based traders founding the firm to attempt to locate a service provider that offers a 'substance package'. Such service providers are understandably sensitive about saying that they are offering 'substance packages' inasmuch, as the clear purpose is to circumvent the tax regulations of other jurisdictions.

Usually, a substance package will include one or more employee contracts, an office rental contract, and other similar services. The service provider will actually provide employees under these contracts to answer the telephone, reconcile invoices, prepare financial statements, and a variety of other administrative functions. Were an investigator or a financial auditor to drop by for a visit, they would find an office with a computer, the name of the company on the door, and a secretary. Failure to make the effort to demonstrate substance in the offshore jurisdiction ensures rejection when a fund applies for offshore tax status. Making the effort, however, does not ensure success. We advise truly investing in creating operations offshore if this is of importance to the would-be manager and we encourage investors to properly due diligence the tax aggressiveness of the manager. The former is the only real way to achieve this goal.

Some jurisdictions, such as Switzerland, are willing to evaluate the evidence on substance and business functioning. They will structure and issue a 'tax ruling' applicable for some years into the future, thereby securing greater certainty of the effectiveness of the substance package. The USA is uncharacteristically clear about its standards for offshore substance.

Funds also endeavour to have offshore directors or other employees who will 'review' and sign documents such as trading strategies, nominations, and brokers' directives. The would-be fund managers should be aware that it is difficult to find honest service providers willing to provide such services. Unless the service provider actually has some knowledge of the underlying commercial business, the process of 'pretending' to be the 'deciding, controlling, or authorizing' party is blatantly untruthful. Offshore service providers may have little to no risk of penalty from the far-distant tax authority in the remote case of being caught in this little game.

Let us consider the disaster scenario. Were the fund to become insolvent or otherwise 'blow up', the signature on the trades will be the unknowledgeable offshore employee, contractor, or director. A wise director will ask himself how it will sound when he must testify: 'No, I really have no clue about these transactions, I only signed off on them to facilitate a tax fraud.' Meanwhile, now that things have gone pear-shaped for the fund, the fund managers will likely claim that they did not have control over the trades that caused the debacle, and that the control was offshore, with those who signed the strategy off.

Control

This worst-case scenario illustrates the most difficult test to satisfy: the control test. Mainland tax authorities (where managers usually operate) will attempt to claim that the investment advisor, through the investment manager, is actually in control of the fund by virtue of his power over the levers of control of the fund. This could result in the determination that the fund itself was subject to taxation in the mainland jurisdiction. Furthermore, the mainland tax authority would argue that the offshore investment manager is either a shell company or at best a 'dependent agent'. In other words, for the mainland tax authority, the brains are really not offshore – they are in the higher-taxed mainland jurisdiction.

In this case, the ruling would be that little of the fund income should be attributable to the offshore jurisdiction. Given that the investment manager will be the recipient of both management fees and performance fees, and that either it or its ultimate shareholders are likely to have a substantial investment of their own money in the fund, the tax status of these offshore structures has significant consequences. Additionally, if the offshore fund is determined to be subject to mainland tax rules, value added tax may be imputed and collected for the 'service' provided by the investment manager to the fund, which is represented by the management fees and performance fees. That means adding an additional 5% to 20% in taxes on top of the fees. Last but not least, the taxes on redemption of shares from a profitable fund will also be significant.

A variety of measures are commonly used to try to demonstrate that in addition to the 'offshore substance', control is actually: (a) offshore and (b) does not lie with the investment manager. The intent is to position the investment manager as just another service provider to the fund. Always keep in mind that legal structures put into place in order to create appearances remain nonetheless legal structures. This means that a legal structure designed to deflect liability to someone else or to give the illusion that another party has control is likely to *actually* transfer some liability *and* control to that entity. To shift the appearance of control implies effectively shifting it. Otherwise, this would be unethical.

We have briefly discussed the role of the founding investor previously. The founding investor's role is particularly relevant when thinking about tax structuring. The founding investor typically buys a few initial shares that do not earn dividends and have no redemption value; however, these shares do have voting rights. These rights usually include: appointment and termination of directors of the fund, changing the articles of association of the fund entity, and winding up the fund. Any effort on the part of the investment manager to create a hidden legal structure that actually gives it control of the 'founding investor' entity will inevitably require fraud or perjury to keep it hidden, and the relationship will ultimately become clear. This approach is not only unethical but illegal. Real control of these critical rights is actually transferred to the founding investor, who must indeed be a trusted party. The founding investor will typically be powerful enough to ultimately dismiss the investment manager. *Remember, the legal appearance of transferring control does indeed transfer control.*

The investment manager should ensure that there are regular board and committee meetings of the fund and the offshore investment manager to review strategy, review performance, approve actions, and discuss future plans. The documentation should build the case that the investment manager is a very important service provider that does not have final control.

Most large or highly profitable investment management groups will be audited in conjunction with their own tax preparation. Doing so will help demonstrate transparency and assist in due diligence conducted by potential investors or regulatory authorities. Auditors of the firm structure are likely to carefully apply these tests of substance and control to determine whether, and in which way, the offshore structure including possibly the fund itself may need to be consolidated into the financials of the firm.

This can have two important consequences: tax authorities receiving copies of the audited financial returns are likely to give significant weight to a determination of a financial auditor that the offshore firm structure is actually a dependent agent and that the fund should be fully consolidated. Further, regulatory bodies may similarly give considerable weight to such an audit determination. This could result in seriously adverse tax consequences for both the firm and the investors. Additionally, it could result in a determination that the offshore fund should additionally be regulated in accordance with the onshore regulations of a particular jurisdiction.

Tax Treatment of the Performance Fee

One additional matter of tax structuring that is of great consequence is the treatment of the performance fee. Depending on the jurisdiction of the fund manager and traders behind the investment manager, the performance fee should be positioned as 'carried interest'. In this way, it would be subject to capital gains tax, which is usually much lower than ordinary income tax. Alternatively, a significant portion of the ordinary income arising from the fees should be attributed to actual intellectual services performed in the offshore jurisdiction.

To illustrate this issue, imagine a US fund manager and a UK-based Spanish trader. A US citizen is taxable on worldwide income and is therefore more likely to attempt to get classification as 'carried interest' subject to capital gains tax. On the contrary, a Spanish trader based in London is likely to claim that a substantial portion of the management and performance fees earned are actually attributable to the valuable service provided by the offshore investment manager entity and therefore should be taxed in the (low-tax or no-tax) offshore jurisdiction. Increasingly, onshore tax and revenue authorities are focusing on this 'foregone' tax revenue. In virtually every mainland jurisdiction, it will get more difficult – not easier – to effectively control an offshore structure and attempt to impute income to the offshore structure, thereby avoiding onshore taxes.

A *special note:* more than one fund manager has invested enormous amounts of time and money in designing a tax structure which will have ongoing requirements for substance packages, travelling to the offshore jurisdiction for meetings, etc. This is time and money invested in creating documentable evidence of offshore substance and control for the purpose of avoiding taxes. However, these taxes might not have been abusively unreasonable to begin with. It is always much easier to optimize the structure within the law and then pay the taxes due. It is very difficult and of questionable ethics to 'give appearances'. One must then walk the thin line that divides tax efficiency from tax fraud. Honest service providers and reputable jurisdictions understand the importance of tax efficiency but are equally eager to avoid being associated with tax fraud.

Investors should be wary of investing in structures that appear to have been too aggressively structured from a tax perspective. In addition to potentially unseen risks to the investors themselves, the investor should not ignore the added operating costs associated with complex tax structuring.

Nor should the investor ignore the potential risk of an investment manager becoming distracted from investing assets due to misguided focus on tax structuring. In the worst-case scenario, the distraction could be fuelled by a need to respond to tax authorities on serious tax-evasion charges. A jailed, distracted, or bankrupt investment manager is a risk to be avoided.

More Contracts

Besides the fund formation documents and PPM (Exhibit B), a start-up hedge fund will need to sign a number of contracts with various service providers including its prime broker(s) and other trading counterparties it may trade OTC derivatives with. Though the suite of contracts that a prime broker will require to on-board a new fund will depend on investment strategy, at a minimum a prime broker will likely require a Prime Brokerage Agreement, an ISDA[9] Master Agreement, and other additional documentation, particularly if OTC derivatives are part of the fund's investment strategy. Additionally, a fund may desire to trade OTC derivatives with other counterparties besides its prime broker, which will require signing additional ISDA Master Agreements, Credit Support Annexes, and other OTC derivatives relates agreements with each of those counterparties.

We highly recommend that a lawyer with experience looking at such contracts assist any hedge fund with reviewing these types of contracts. Like many legal agreements, no one really looks at them when things are going well; however, it is when things are not going well that the provision in such agreement can become critical. The fallout from Lehman Brothers bankruptcy during the GFC is a recent, high-profile example of the importance of understanding the mechanisms embedded within such documentation. Though not comprehensive by any means (and please consult with your legal counsel) some key areas, inter alia, to consider when negotiating an ISDA Master Agreement are: cross-default provisions, net asset value triggers, events of default/termination events and how they will be treated if they occur, taxation issues, collateral terms, and ensuring consistency between the ISDA Master Agreement and other agreements the fund may have signed.

Be Nice To Your Lawyer

An investment of time and strategic thinking at the beginning of the journey will minimize legal and tax issues down the road. The legal and tax issues

---

[9]ISDA stands for the International Swaps and Derivatives Association, which is the trade organization that sets the standards for how OTC derivative transactions are transacted and documented.

that need to be addressed for new hedge funds are not cookie-cutter but very specific to a fund's particular investment strategy, the jurisdictions it operates in geographically, and the nationalities of its employees. All of the above needs to be considered within the context of ever-evolving bodies of law and regulatory requirements, further adding to the complexity.

The information in this chapter is designed to provide a broad framework to help fund founders think about key legal issues as they engage legal counsel, accountants, and regulators in establishing a successful new fund. Lastly, we also encourage you to channel your inner Shakespeare and be sure to partner with quality legal counsel that can help you navigate the legal process of forming and managing a fund.

Bibliography

Law firms and other professional service firms active in the investment management and investment funds space regularly disseminate updates on new laws and regulations. These updates are a good way to stay abreast of changes. Additionally, regulators such as the US SEC offer updates via e-mail subscription for free.

Carreno, F., McGrade, L., and Page, A.N. (2012) *Hedge Funds: A Practical Global Handbook to the Law and Regulation*. Globe Law & Business: London.

Morgan Lewis & Bockius LLP (2012) *Hedge Fund Deskbook: Legal and Practical Guidance for the Dodd–Frank New Era*. Thomson Reuters: New York.

Nowak, G. (2009) *Hedge Fund Agreement Line by Line: A User's Guide to LLC Operating Contracts*. Thomson Reuters: New York.

Shartsis Friese LLP (2006) *U.S. Regulation of Hedge Funds*. American Bar Association: Chicago, IL.

Zetzsche, D. (2012) *The Alternative Investment Fund Managers Directive: European Regulation of Investment Funds*. Kluwer Law International: Dordrecht.

Chapter 7

Service Providers

*A wife lasts only for the length of the marriage, but an
ex-wife is there for the rest of your life.*
Woody Allen after his first divorce

Introduction

As has been described throughout the book thus far, a successful investment management enterprise will not only have consistent investment
performance but also be built on a solid business foundation. When considering the management aspect of the investment management enterprise, one
lens to use is that a substantial part of the management function is to manage relationships with service providers. These relationships are represented
through a series of contracts that the investment management enterprise
signs with a variety of service providers.

In this chapter, we cover important points to remember as you deal with
individual service providers. The advice offered here is not meant to be
exhaustive. Indeed, to propose that it could be would be foolhardy on our
part. Each fund, each strategy, each individual manager will have varying
needs depending on the type of investment strategy they wish to employ,
the jurisdictions in which they operate, and based on how much they can
afford or are willing to pay for particular services. As can easily be inti-
mated, selecting service providers is a very *sui generis* experience for each
investment management enterprise.

Additionally, although service provider relationships will be formalized
via legal contracts, it is important to remember that first and foremost when
selecting service providers one is making a decision based on capabilities
and relationships. Invariably, there will be people at various service providers that a founder or chief operating officer of a fund will click with more
than others. This is human nature and should not be ignored. That said,
even if a particular service provider meets the 'fit' test, that service provider

may not provide the right capabilities. Thus, fit and capabilities should be viewed in conjunction with one another.

Long-Term Relationship: Service Providers and Marriage

Wisely selecting the right service provider for a particular investment management enterprise cannot be overemphasized. Entering into a relationship with a service provider should be viewed as akin to getting married. As a happy marriage provides blessings to both parties, similarly a relationship between a service provider and a hedge fund should also ideally be both long term and beneficial to both sides. Conversely, as a divorce can frequently lead to acrimony and bitterness for both sides, similarly a relationship between a service provider and a hedge fund that deteriorates can also be a source of pain for both parties.

There are a few reasons for this. At a basic level, there is a signalling effect that comes into play. Newly launched funds want to be associated with reputable service providers since they provide the fund with a measure of credibility, particularly when the fund founder and his or her team may not have much of a track record or are otherwise lacking substantial experience. Being associated with a well-known prime broker, law firm, administrator, audit firm, etc. can help resolve any initial doubt that a potential investor or regulator might have had if the fund was instead involved with a group of service providers that were not well known.

The flip side of the above is that service providers also want to be associated with reputable funds, particularly those funds that they feel may perform well, grow in size, and/or otherwise be considered high profile. A successful fund will not only generate revenue for the service provider but, if the fund does indeed become high profile, also provide vicarious marketing for the service provider, which will hopefully lead to other funds in the future seeking out the service provider.

Readily apparent from the above is that when things are proceeding to plan, the relationship between a fund and a service provider should be mutually beneficial. As the fund grows and enjoys success, service providers by extension should also be beneficiaries of that success. There is a saying: 'A rising tide raises all ships', and this is appropriate here. A successful fund should lead to positive relationships with its service providers.

In the event that a relationship between a fund and its service providers begins deteriorating, this poses quite a dilemma for both the fund and its service providers. These negative situations can arise from poor market conditions, such as during the 2008 GFC, when both funds and some service providers might have been under distress. Of course this is an extreme case, but even more normal conditions can be equally problematic – when a fund is not getting the service it expects or requires from a particular service provider, this can pose quite a significant issue. For example, if a fund that utilizes a particular strategy relies on its prime broker's ability to offer a specified amount of leverage at a particular price, and it can no longer receive that required service, a fundamental problem has arisen that affects the ability of the investment management enterprise to successfully implement its investment strategy. At this point, a review of the relationship may be in order.

Another important point to consider when both engaging and altering service providers is the impact that such a change may have on investors. As a general rule, investors prefer consistency. In our experience, the importance of this rule corresponds to the size of the institution and the amount of capital they can allocate to a fund. The bigger the institution and the larger their prospective cheque, the more important consistency is viewed. As a fund dealing with these types of investor, you do not want to give them (or any investor for that matter) an excuse to either not allocate to your fund or to question if they should maintain their investment. The competitiveness of the fundraising landscape is such that you should minimize any reason an institution may have to question the wisdom of investing in your fund. One of these red flags is switching service providers without good reason and particularly doing so with any sort of regularity.

Service Providers: Who and Where?

The way a particular investment management enterprise is structured will determine how the relationships with the service providers are constructed. The reason for this is that the investment management enterprise will likely be a different legal entity (and likely in a different jurisdiction) from the actual funds that are related to the investment management enterprise. Thus, the service providers for the fund and for the investment management enterprise may need to be different.

For example, a particular investment firm might be incorporated in the UK but its constituent funds may be in offshore jurisdictions such as the Cayman Islands or Jersey. In this situation, at a minimum, the UK entity will probably have a legal advisor and an auditor. Additionally, the offshore funds would have an auditor, fund administrator, custodian, legal advisor, prime broker, other ancillary brokers, and probably a registered office service of some sort. In most situations, the auditor for the UK entity and the offshore funds is probably the same company, though the actual employees doing the auditing might be in different branches (e.g., UK auditors conducting the annual audit for the UK entity while auditors affiliated with the offshore branch office undertake the annual audit for the offshore funds). Furthermore, it is quite common for onshore counsel (in this case UK counsel) to be different from offshore counsel (e.g., Cayman Islands counsel).

The simple example offered above highlights the importance of identifying which entities may need which service. When setting up relationships between the investment management enterprise and its service providers, it is important to keep the nature and geography of the relationships clear. Once operations are established and everything is set up, the structure of these relationships will likely become imprinted on your memory but early on, the relationships can be slightly confusing.

Negotiate, Negotiate, Negotiate

The relationships with service providers are represented by legal contracts. Admittedly, these agreements are not as interesting to read as the newest *New York Times* bestseller, but they are incredibly important. During good times, when everyone is happy because the markets are doing well, the legal documents a fund signs with its service providers will likely collect dust on a shelf or be stored dormant on a hard drive somewhere in the office. It is when the markets maybe are not doing well or when the fund is not performing as desired that some of these agreements will become critical. On that day, you do not want to wish you had spent more time reading and negotiating an agreement with a service provider instead of having picked up your favourite book.

At the risk of being pedantic, we point out that it is important to read everything. We encourage you to engage internal or external legal counsel to review your legal documents. Even if you do have legal counsel review your agreements, it is still important for the firm founder or other senior member of the management team to read through the documents and 'sign off'. If there are parts of an agreement you do not understand, have both your legal counsel and the service provider explain those provisions to you to ensure that: (1) you understand everything correctly; and (2) everyone else is on the same page when it comes to interpretation of the agreement.

After working with numerous service providers over the years, what we have come to realize is that many are not much more knowledgeable than the clients they are serving. This is not an indictment on the intelligence or diligence of the employees at service providers, but a natural result of turnover in the industry as well as a great deal of legal and regulatory change. Consequently, a good number of employees at service providers do not have the institutional knowledge required to explain why certain terms are in an agreement or why a certain process is conducted the way it is. Normally, they have inherited a legacy process and are basically paid to have as many clients as possible follow that work flow. Given that, do not be afraid to explore or ask questions if something seems amiss, does not seem to make sense, or does not otherwise comport with the way you understand the markets or a particular process.

Once everything is read and understood, do not hesitate to negotiate the terms that you feel are important to your business. For the most part, the draft agreements that service providers send to their clients are template agreements that are broadly drafted and generally very protective to the service provider. Inevitably, there will be funds that will sign the agreements as they are, without any pushback or questioning. As a general matter, we recommend that this not be you.

Ultimately, you may sign the agreement as it is, but this should only be done after careful consideration and after any clarifications have been made. Negotiating with service providers should not be thought of as a zero-sum game, it is not and frankly the negotiations should not be adversarial in nature. Through questioning and pushback, you are trying to create a win–win situation that makes sense for your fund(s). This process of reviewing agreements is just one step in the relationship-building process of what will hopefully be a long-term relationship that is mutually beneficial for both sides (i.e., a happy marriage).

We advise that you approach each agreement with the mind-set that everything is open to negotiation. In reality, this may not be the case but for terms that are particularly important for your fund(s), do explore if there is any flexibility. Funds with a bit more star power due to the reputation of the team, funds that seem like they might grow assets quickly due to investor interest, or funds that appear to be a potential source of high fees will generally have more leverage in their negotiating position. Additionally, if the particular service provider you are negotiating with is aggressively trying to expand its market share or is otherwise aggressively competing for clients, these types of factor will also potentially increase your fund's bargaining position.

One final point before departing this section is that as you build out the investment management enterprise, with perhaps multiple entities including managed accounts, multiple funds, and other products, there may be opportunities to achieve economies of scale in the type of pricing you receive from your service providers. For example, if your fund enterprise maintains the same auditor for all its group companies, then it may be easier to negotiate a more competitive price for the audit of the group companies as a whole, as opposed to trying to negotiate price on a piecemeal basis, entity by entity. This should be kept in mind as the business is started and hopefully continues to grow.

Service?

A good relationship with the right service providers will make the challenges of starting a new investment management enterprise significantly easier. Service providers are advisers and partners that can guide the inexperienced founder through the myriad processes and piles of paperwork that are necessary to navigate in order to successfully launch a new firm.

At a minimum, fund service provider groups will included the following types of firm:

- Administrator
- Custodian[10]
- Auditor
- Directors
- Execution and Clearing Brokers
- Prime Broker
- Legal Counsel
- Registered Office Services.

The work of a fund's administrator covers a wide scope of activities. An administrator's work includes, but is not limited to: fund accounting, NAV computation, maintaining share registry, anti-money laundering and related compliance, subscription and redemption processing, preparing annual reports, and other services for fund managers. Besides a fund's prime broker, an administrator is the service provider who will work with the fund most closely and serve as an interface with investors. Thus, it is important to find an administrator that not only offers the necessary services but one whom you feel comfortable having as a long-term partner.

---

[10]Following new regulations in Europe, a custodian is no longer required, only a depositary. Though many hedge funds may continue to use the services of a custodian as they are often affiliated with a hedge fund's prime broker.

A custodian is a financial institution that holds and safeguards the fund's assets. A custodian can hold cash or the securities of the fund. Depending on the size of the fund's assets and the different assets being held, a fund may rely on more that one custodian. A custodian may be an entity that is related to a fund's service provider. For example, many fund's use a custodian that is affiliated with the fund's prime broker. Alternatively, a fund may choose to use a custodian (or custodians) that are independent, stand-alone entities (i.e., not part of a global bank that has a prime brokerage arm) or a custodian that may not be stand-alone but is independent of its existing service providers.

A fund's auditors are principally responsible for the preparation of annual reports and conducting annual audits to confirm the financial integrity of the company and to help detect fraud or other related issues. Going through the audit process is normally not the most enjoyable experience, however, it is an important part of good corporate governance and a basic component of being a responsible steward of client assets.

Though not technically service providers, the selection of directors is another constituency that needs to be considered as one begins a new fund or investment management enterprise. Directors are either executive directors or non-executive directors. An executive director is a senior member (an 'executive') of the fund or investment management enterprise and also serves on its board of directors. A non-executive director is an external person that serves on the board and is not an employee of the fund or firm. Both executive and non-executive directors have a fiduciary duty to represent the interests of the shareholders of the respective entity they sit on the board of directors for. Ideally, directors serve as strategic advisors and partners that help the new enterprise grow as opposed to simply being a rubber stamp for whatever the management of the fund or firm wants to do.

When trading commodities, it is important to identify proper execution and clearing brokers for a prospective strategy or product. Which exchanges does our product trade on? Will the trades be exchange-cleared OTC derivatives? Do we need to be able to take physical delivery? These may be simple questions for the commodity trader, but the answers need to be built into the decision calculus when thinking about exchange and clearing brokers as well as when selecting service providers more broadly. Ideally, you are able to partner with service providers who understand commodities and how they are traded.

Generally, a fund's prime broker will be its most important service provider. A prime broker can help a new fund get up and running as well as provide the knowledge, network, and expertise to prevent the new fund from making too many mistakes in the early days. Prime brokers will likely serve as a fund's execution broker and offer leverage on transactions if needed for a fund's strategy. Additionally, almost all prime brokers provide a suite of value-added service, including capital introduction, business consulting, and pre-fund launch services. A prime broker will also provide its clients with access to its research capability.

Legal counsel has been discussed earlier in this chapter and other places in this book. Many investment management enterprises will have both onshore and offshore legal counsel, depending on how the enterprise is structured. Legal costs can quickly add up, so it is important to work with legal advisors that understand the business and will complete work in an efficient manner. Related to legal counsel, due to increasing regulatory oversight and new regulations, many firms in the alternative investments universe are turning to compliance and regulatory consultants to assist them in fulfilling their obligations in multiple jurisdictions.

For legal reasons, most new funds will likely be required to have registered offices. Often times, this can be an additional service that might be offered by a law firm or other service provider. The use of registered offices is important when an investment firm has legal entities in different jurisdictions.

How to Choose?

Selecting a service provider can be difficult. When a new investment management enterprise is started, many service providers will be eager to pitch their services. They will all extol the virtues of their firm and how much experience they have and how successful they have been. Most of these people will seem very likeable and could potentially be great partners. In this marketing milieu, we offer a few suggestions to consider. Depending on the specific needs of your particular firm, you may need to add to the list below, but we feel this is a good starting point to begin the filtering process when selecting new service providers.

For each of the service providers you may be considering, as objectively as possible, please consider:

- Brand value and reputation of the prospective service provider (e.g., Goldman Sachs as a prime broker is much more reputable than an unknown bank in a country known for money laundering).
- Cost: both in the short and long term. Additionally, if your business may receive tangibly better service, which is necessary to be successful, then it may make sense to pay more for a particular service.

- Experience and capability. What are a service provider's capabilities? How successful have they been in working with firms that might have a similar strategy to yours?
- Growth. Can this service provider grow with the business or will an upgrade be necessary once a certain AUM is reached or a decision is made to diversify into other products or markets?
- Attitude. Does the service provider in question genuinely have a desire to serve their client? Do they want to be a partner? Will they be there when things get difficult?
- Flexibility. Though most of the service providers you will likely interact with will be global companies with set procedures, it may be useful to explore how flexible they are in accommodating specific needs you may have. For example, you may require specific legal language in your service agreement or prefer interacting directly with key personnel or legal personnel at the service provider instead of through a sales contact. If a service provider is willing to be reasonably flexible then set-up and ongoing management will likely be a bit smoother.

Final Thoughts

Finally, remember that service providers are there to help you be successful. They are there to help prevent headaches not provide them. That said, as the relationship develops you may need to provide them with feedback to help modulate the working relationship to ensure it is as smooth as possible. Our hope is that as you work with the right service provider partners your investment management enterprise will mirror Woody Allen's illustrious cinematic career and not end in a series of divorces.

Bibliography

Aikman, J.S. (2010) *When Prime Brokers Fail: The Unheeded Risk to Hedge Funds, Banks, and the Financial Industry.* John Wiley & Sons: Hoboken, NJ.

Berman, M. (ed.) (2007) *Hedge Funds and Prime Brokers.* Risk Books: London.

Strachman, D.A. (2012) *The Fundamentals of Hedge Fund Management: How to Successfully Launch and Operate a Hedge Fund.* John Wiley & Sons: Chichester.

Wilson, R. (2011) *The Hedge Fund Book: A Training Manual for Professionals and Capital Raising Executives.* John Wiley & Sons: Hoboken, NJ.

PART IV

RUNNING THE BUSINESS

Chapter 8

Fundraising

Show me the money!
Tom Cruise, in the movie *Jerry Maguire*

The survival of any investment firm is contingent upon raising capital and generating acceptable returns from that capital. Outside a few very rare exceptions, most funds will constantly be concerned with either raising additional capital or ensuring that capital remains invested. The fundraising process is a marathon that is sometimes tedious, but must be run well for a fund to succeed since the best investor in the world without capital is nothing more than a spectator. This chapter draws on our experiences of raising capital for multiple funds. We learned these lessons the hard way. With some of these lessons in mind, hopefully the road will be smoother for you.

The relationship between a fund and its investors can take many shapes. In fact, most investors would argue that the way in which funds approach and manage their investors is a key aspect that varies most noticeably from one fund to another. Some funds view their investors as necessary evils, or as objects of marketing and public relations management. The most productive fund–investor relationships, however, are those in which funds treat investors as business partners and foster collaborative relationships. Furthermore, successful funds always treat their investors as respected and appreciated clients.

Although there is often more investor money available than a wise fund manager requires, the reality is that not all investment money is equally desirable. Certain types of investors suit certain types of funds better than others because certain funds are able to more easily satisfy particular investor needs (e.g., lower return volatility, future capacity to meaningfully increase invested assets, etc.). Accordingly, a fund manager must analyse what the characteristics of their investment offering are. A fund manager trying to attract an investor that may not be a good fit can waste precious time. The fund manager must avoid spending excessive amounts of time maintaining specific investor relationships for the wrong reasons, and even more importantly the fund manager must avoid successfully attracting investors who may bring unnecessary volatility to the asset pool or heightened risk of legal and regulatory action.

First, we will discuss strategic investor portfolio design, examine the key characteristics of investors that determine their attractiveness to a fund, review where each of the main types of investor stands with regard to these key features, and formulate an adequate strategy for selecting investors depending on the 'lifecycle stage' of a fund. Second, we shall describe the practical aspects of investor acquisition, how to market the fund to potential investors, including identification of possible investors, organization of investor meetings or 'road shows', and preparation of 'pitch' material. Finally, we will examine how to manage a successful investor maintenance programme, reviewing how different investors require different forms and frequency of communication, and dissimilar packaging of both good and bad news.

Strategic Investor Portfolio Design

Types of Investor

The main types of investor are ranked below in order of institutionalization. By institutionalization we mean the degree to which an investor has fixed, well-defined methods of investment evaluation as well as guidelines around their investment strategy. The ordering itself is not sacrosanct but purely based on our experience and we readily admit that other people may have had different fundraising experiences.

A. Sovereign wealth funds: funds backed by national governments that manage the investment of government-owned assets.
B. Fund of hedge funds: funds that do not invest directly in any asset class, but rather invest in a portfolio of hedge funds (we include bank-owned fund of funds and asset management arms of banks in this category).
C. Endowment funds: funds which invest assets amassed by institutions such as universities – often through donations.
D. Pension and insurance funds: pension funds that invest pooled pension plan contributions in order to finance the resulting pension plan benefits, and insurance funds which invest the float or other balance-sheet assets of insurance firms to fund their liabilities.

E. Family office funds: funds that invest the assets of very wealthy families.
F. Corporate pension funds: funds that invest the assets of employees of large companies.
G. Ultra high-net-worth individuals (UHNWI): very wealthy individuals who invest directly in diverse asset classes.
H. Retail customers: individuals who invest small amounts of assets that get aggregated into larger pools prior to being invested, by aggregators such as banks.

Key Investor Profile Characteristics

The key investor profile characteristics that are most relevant in determining their attractiveness to a fund are the following (by 'preferences' we also often mean 'requirements'; depending on how 'set in stone' these preferences are – there are typically – but not always – exceptions to the rule around some of them):

1. Fund manager track record and reputation expectations.

2. Investor preferences on fund capacity.

3. Volatility appetite/risk tolerance.

4. Investor preferences on legal and operational attributes of the fund.

5. Investor preferences on investment asset class characteristics.

6. Investor preferences on fund investment strategy.

7. Investor regulatory, tax, and legal characteristics.

8. Investor preferences on investment strategy visibility and transparency.

9. Investor preferences on composition of investors in the fund.

10. Sophistication of investor.

11. Investor acquisition and maintenance ease.

12. Investor preferences of liquidity.

13. Fee structure and fee payment schedule.

   We will now briefly examine each key investor profile characteristic before discussing how the main types of investor stack up against them.

   1. **Fund manager record and reputation expectations.** All investors value an exceptional track record and reputation. In fact, investors will only vary in the degree to which they require the track record to be proven

by hard data, and the degree to which a given reputation must be widely shared among market players, former colleagues, former employers, etc.

The perceived experience of a fund manager is one of the most important factors for investors when determining a fund's attractiveness, and therefore defines the ease with which a fund will be able to raise and maintain capital. Would-be fund managers will often find it difficult to prove their own track record if they have been trading at a bank's prop desk or under the control of a larger fund (versus a standalone fund). For example, if a trader has been a high-level employee at a trading company or fund, investors can more easily verify his/her track record. Investors will find it harder to confirm the track record of former lower-level employees at a similar company or even a former senior employee at a more opaque company such as a large utility trading desk. In addition, there may be regulatory, legal, and competitive reasons that prevent a fund manager from providing evidence to support their claimed track record.

Therefore, investors also place great importance on a second form of supporting evidence: reputation. Investors will 'talk to the market' in order to build a picture of an aspiring fund manager's reputation in the market. More experienced investors will assess not only their reputation concerning performance, but also other aspects such as behaviour under stress, level of risk taking, and standing as an employee and/or employer. Furthermore, if a trader has no physical evidence of a track record, or must disguise it for legal reasons, only a stellar reputation will give investors confidence in its veracity.

Investors whose investment decision making is concentrated and investment guidelines are less codified or regulated will be more flexible around whether or not a track record is essential and the degree to which it must be supported by written evidence or reputational anecdotes. Investors who are focused on new or less experienced fund managers may also be more permissive of inconclusive track records. Additionally, it might be helpful to mention that certain investors may be willing (or even prefer) to set-up a managed account given the improved control and transparency compared to investing in a co-mingled fund vehicle. This option may be worth considering for both the new as well as experienced fund manager.

2. **Investor preferences on fund capacity.** Energy markets have not been around for long compared with, for instance, equity markets. In fact, if we compare Europe's largest energy exchange, the EEX, with the London Stock Exchange, the EEX is considerably smaller.

As we have seen earlier, the size of different non-oil energy commodities markets varies considerably, and they are to some extent location specific. This means that the maximum amount of capital that can be invested in certain markets and in certain products within those markets is not infinite. In such markets, there comes a point when the positions of one single fund can begin affecting the market dynamics (and become relatively clear to competitors). A fund manager must assess the maximum capital he will be able to utilize before individual trading activity starts to influence markets or reveals the fund's positions to competitors. We call this amount the maximum amount of deployable assets.

Investors with considerable assets under management will require assurance that the markets a fund trades will have sufficient capacity to absorb subsequent investments beyond the initial allocation. Furthermore, some investors will require that a fund explicitly reserve capacity for that investor within the fund (in essence, reserving a portion of the maximum amount of deployable assets for them).

3. **Volatility appetite/risk tolerance.** Appetite for risk varies from one type of investor to another. So does their ability to understand the risk implicit in their investment, and hence the potential volatility. Volatility is, very simply, the rate of change of asset prices,[11] and some investors dislike (or may not be used to) the monthly reports of a fund showing significant deviations from what they expect monthly 'average' returns to be. For this reason, fund managers must be aware of their potential investors' volatility appetite, as an investor with a low volatility appetite may find significant swings in returns on a monthly basis unnerving, causing unease. This may translate into time-consuming 'hand-holding' sessions with investors and ultimately possibly lead to redemptions. Volatility in a fund's performance will not be appreciated by investors if it is unexpected. It is therefore crucial to ensure that an investor's expectations are properly managed. Investors will not mind if returns are potentially volatile if they are expecting them to be volatile given the high volatility of the underlying. The key is that investors be aware of this when deciding to invest.

---

[11]You may come across a distinction between 'realized' and 'implied' volatility. 'Realized' volatility looks at the actual movements of prices in financial markets. 'Implied' volatility is in essence 'backed out' from option prices. In option pricing, the expected forward looking volatility is one of the factors that determines price, and so options prices indirectly reflect expected or 'implied' volatility.

4. **Fund legal and operational attribute preferences.** Most investors have established guidelines around what legal and operational characteristics a fund must meet. The degree to which these guidelines are codified are a function of how sophisticated the investor is, the degree to which it is subject to regulation, its size (codification usually comes with size), and how concentrated the ownership of the assets are (the more owners an investor vehicle has, the more it will tend to codify investment guidelines). The degree to which these guidelines are fixed depends also on the level of pertinent regulation, and on the degree of control the investor exercises upon his own assets. For example, UHNWIs will be able to be more flexible with applying guidelines, which are more preferences than requirements given that little or no regulation applies to their investment decisions, and they have full control of their assets. On the contrary, a government pension fund will have very strict guidelines fixed by law or other regulations that are inflexible requirements.

There are a large number of legal and operational attributes that are examined by investors throughout the due diligence process. Certain attributes will be equally important to all investors, and all investors will be looking for the same attribute. Other attributes, however, will be a regulatory requirement for some investors and an inconsequential characteristic to others. For this reason, in the analysis by investor type, we focus on those attributes which are most important to each. These attributes include, yet are not limited to: the legal and tax jurisdiction of the fund, the voting rights associated with ownership of fund shares, whether the fund is publicly listed or not, the quality of the service providers, and the independence of the risk management function.

5. **Fund investment asset class characteristic preferences.** Although within the world of hedge fund vehicles most trading is done in financial products such as energy futures, the size of the physical energy markets is in fact larger than the financial markets. A fund may decide to trade assets that are difficult to value or not exchange traded. The features of the products in which a fund invests will determine the types of investor it is most attractive to, and those it becomes ineligible to.

There are several dimensions along which investors will assess the asset classes a fund invests in: the nature of the asset (equity, security, future, option, or physical); whether the asset class is publicly or privately traded (and if publicly traded, whether it is publicly traded on a recognized exchange); some investors will consider the asset represents an 'ethical' investment; what the time horizon of the asset is; whether the assets can be valued by market mechanisms, etc.

6. **Fund investment strategy preferences.** Understanding what products, strategies, and markets an investor is looking for will allow fund managers to focus on investors who are more likely to invest. A fund manager must evaluate if his or her strategy complements or duplicates investments an investor already holds. Additionally, a fund manager would do well to assess whether investors have preferences around the minimum markets they wish their funds to cover in order to achieve diversification and the existence of any products and markets they may have a policy against investing in (e.g., CO_2 emissions).

7. **Investor regulatory, tax, and legal characteristics.** Whilst all investor profile characteristics help determine how attractive a given investor is for a fund, their regulatory, tax, and legal characteristics carry greater importance. First, the regulatory restrictions of certain investors may result in the fund itself coming under regulatory scrutiny. For example, the SEC only allows funds to manage a maximum of 25% of their AUM in ERISA money without becoming liable to SEC regulation. Second, taxation characteristics of investors may bring funds under foreign tax jurisdictions. Third, some investors are more prone to litigation in the case of perceived breach of investment contracts, especially in times of poor performance. This litigiousness is also linked to regulatory characteristics, as some investors may be obliged to pursue legal action in scenarios of fraud or other wrongdoing. Greater exposure to regulatory intervention and/or lawsuits requires funds to dedicate more time and resources to managing this risk.

8. **Fund investment strategy transparency preferences.** Investors may have policies around how much investment strategy or trading information a fund supplies them. Although some investors may be happy with understanding the types of position a fund puts on in the market – their size, length, or correlation – others will only invest in a fund if they are given full visibility of all investments and trades, on a position-by-position basis. For example, some investors will only invest through managed accounts that give full real-time visibility down to position-level granularity. A fund manager must evaluate whether he is comfortable with sharing details of his trading strategy, including current positions, with investors. The risks to consider include the potential of this information being used against him or her, or leaked to competitors.

9. **Composition of fund investor preferences.** The more institutionalized an investor, the stricter their guidelines around maximum fund stakeholding. Most investors will have policies pertaining to the maximum percentage of the assets in a fund they want to own. Owning a majority stakeholding in a fund may have legal, tax, and regulatory implications, and it is therefore an important limitation for many investors.

10. **Investor sophistication.** Admittedly, investor sophistication is a relatively subjective concept. Having said that, it is difficult to argue against the observation that investors range from the very knowledgeable to the very ignorant – and that is not necessarily a bad thing. Energy commodity hedge funds for one are not as mainstream as – for instance – equity funds, and there are many investors who are ignorant about the intricacies of energy commodity investing because they have not previously studied the space. Fund managers must therefore evaluate investors with respect to their level of familiarity with the energy commodity space, as some investors will require more education on the subject than others. The implication is that investors will act differently depending on their sophistication, from the acquisition to the maintenance stage. As a function of their understanding of the market, some customers may overreact to periods of volatility, require more explanation about current strategy or performance, etc. All these concerns will translate into additional time and resource investment on the part of the fund manager, who must learn to manage investors with varying degrees of sophistication.

11. **Acquisition and ease of maintenance** (linked to **investor sophistication** above). Funds must consider the fact that some investors may require more sophisticated and costly marketing efforts. This may be due to their level of sophistication, since a less sophisticated investor may need to be educated on what energy commodity funds really do. It may also have to do with the fact that they are based considerably far away from the fund, and a lot of travel is involved in acquiring them. It may, however, not have anything to do with sophistication at all. Investors vary in how meticulous they are in their investment appraisals, how lengthy and demanding their due diligence procedures are, and how often they wish to be updated with trading developments. Fund managers should assess how resource- and time-intensive the acquisition and retention of different investors will be, and plan their marketing efforts accordingly. Of course, there may be trade-offs between short- and long-term objectives, as an investor who is more costly to acquire may also have longer investment horizons and therefore remain an investor for a longer time period.

12. **Liquidity preferences.** The liquidity offered by funds can be a make-or-break feature for certain types of investors. As we have seen, liquidity is a function of the redemption terms, which include the timing of redemption days (when redemptions are permitted – usually at the end of every quarter), the redemption notice period (the minimum time period that must elapse between redemption notification and the redemption day), and the redemption gate (a cap on the percentage of AUM or individual

investor money invested that can be redeemed). Investors who are not ultimately the owners of the capital they invest, and pool the assets of others (such as fund of funds do), will only invest in funds whose liquidity terms mirror their own. For example, a fund of funds with quarterly liquidity for its own investors may not afford to have their capital invested in funds locked up for longer than a quarter, as they may have to return it within three months if their investors redeem. This point is less of a problem for investors who are investing their own assets, such as sovereign wealth funds or UHNWIs, but it nonetheless remains an important consideration.

13. **Fund fee structure and fee payment schedule preferences.** It is easy to overestimate the importance of fees to investors as they are often a subject for negotiation, whilst other aspects such as operational robustness or liquidity terms are not. Having said this, all investors will not be willing to negotiate on fees, or pay fees that are higher than what is deemed to be a reasonable 'industry average', unless the competitive advantage or 'edge' of the fund warrants it. Investors who are less worried about motivating risk taking or who are sophisticated enough to argue against management fees being charged for average market level performance will insist that a greater portion of the fees be biased towards performance fees. Indeed, some investors may not want to pay management fees at all. In addition to the fee level, investors will be particularly concerned with the payment schedule of these fees. For example, some investors prefer to pay performance fees annually, to increase the exposure of fund managers (in the shape of unpaid performance fees) thus creating incentives for responsible risk taking.

Key Investor Profile Characteristics by Investor Type

A. **Sovereign wealth funds.** Sovereign wealth funds (SWFs) are state-owned investment companies that manage and invest national savings. SWFs are usually managed central banks, national investment management organizations, or national pension funds. In essence, SWFs are tasked with investing current account surpluses – which in most cases are generated by the export of plentiful natural resources, particularly oil and gas.

The level of transparency SWFs offer varies greatly, with some being very open about their investment strategy, guidelines, and actual investments, and others being very secretive and opaque. Norway leads the way in terms of openness, with its 'Government Pension Fund – Global' (formerly 'The Government Petroleum Fund') having become the leading openness benchmark.

Most SWFs invest in both financial and non-financial assets, and are perhaps slightly more on the longer-term time horizon end of the spectrum. SWFs tend to prefer portfolio-type foreign investments to direct foreign investments, and have increasingly been investing in hedge funds. There is growing concern that some SWFs are motivated by non-financial objectives, however, this should not impact their participation in hedge fund markets.

The investor profile characteristics of any given SWF are a function, primarily, of how transparent they are. More opaque SWFs will tend to be more flexible in their requirements, given that the public cannot scrutinize their decisions. Transparent SWFs will have more numerous, demanding, and clearly established guidelines, and will not compromise on their requirements.

B. **Fund of hedge funds.** Fund of hedge funds (FoFs) are pooled investment vehicles that allow investors to diversify their investment across a number of individual hedge funds. FoFs that invest in only one type of strategy, asset class, or industry are known as single-strategy or niche FoFs and those that invest across a range are known as multi-strategy FoFs. FoFs are usually more flexible with respect to a fund manager's track record.

FoFs monitor performance more closely, generally on at least a quarterly, if not monthly, basis, given their underlying clients can usually redeem on a quarter's notice. As a result, they are known to be less 'sticky' money as investors in FoFs are frequently 'less sticky' themselves. Fund managers tend to have an aversion to this type of money given that lack of stickiness can put the liquidity of the fund at risk and force unwanted position closing in a worst-case scenario.

C. **Endowment funds.** Endowment funds invest assets amassed usually through donations, such as for a university.

D. **Pension funds and insurance funds.** These are funds that invest pooled pension plan contributions in order to pay for future financial obligations that the pension will have to pay to its contributors and funds that invest insurance firm assets.

E. **Family office funds.** These funds invest the assets of very wealthy families; they can be single-family offices (SFOs) or cater to a number of families as multi-family offices (MFOs).

F. **Corporate pension funds.** These funds invest the assets of employees of large companies.

G. **Ultra high-net-worth individuals.** These are individuals with very considerable assets who invest directly in diverse asset classes.

H. **Retail customers.** These are individuals who invest small amounts of assets that get aggregated into larger pools prior to being invested, by aggregators such as banks.

Start-up Lifecycle Analysis and Investor Portfolio Development

When assessing or planning the design of an investor portfolio, a fund manager must consider what point the fund is at and the way in which to develop the investor base moving forward. There are three main stages:

Stage 1: Pre-launch.

Stage 2: Early Stage (less than one year trading).

Stage 3: Late Stage (more than one year trading). Important to note that for the purpose of a start-up, we characterize 'Stage 3: Late Stage' as more than one year trading. In the context of a fund's total life cycle and not just start-up stages, one year of trading is still very young for a hedge fund.

Treating strategic investor portfolio building as a process made up of distinct stages enables a fund manager to create a structured fundraising strategy and properly focus fundraising efforts. The lifecycle a fund is in will determine which investors a fund should focus on, because a fund's lifecycle often underpins the perceived attractiveness of a fund for the vast majority of investors.

One important distinction to make is that a fund can be in a different lifecycle from its fund manager. Although a fund manager may set up a new fund, he or she may have been managing an existing fund for a considerable amount of time and have a demonstrable, easily documentable, and well-known track record. This would mean that although the fund is technically a pre-launch fund (being marketed as a fund which is not yet launched), he or she is very much an established fund manager, and is lending established credibility to the new fund. When we analyse a fund's lifecycle in this section, we do so from the point of view of a 'new' fund manager.

A 'new' fund manager is someone who has previously not single-handedly managed a fund that can be identified as a standalone fund, and which has its own demonstrable track record. With this definition, fund managers that may have been managing a fund within a larger trading platform – a large energy utility, or investment bank for example – would come under the heading of 'new' fund manager. The one caveat to this definition is that if a fund manager who has worked within a larger organization is able to prove that a given performance track record is attributable to him, he may be able to use this in the way an experienced standalone fund manager would.

Pre-Launch

The investors most likely to invest in pre-launch funds are investors who believe they have a certain edge in this particular form of investment, namely pre-launch investing – also known as seeding. Certain FoFs and high-net-worth individuals are the investors most likely to be pre-launch investors.

Traditionally, late-stage investors tend to invest earlier and earlier given increasing competitiveness among investors for certain types of fund. Many outperforming energy commodity hedge funds are often oversubscribed and are closed to new investors who did not get in early enough. Furthermore, there is a perception that pre-launch or early-stage investing has a higher prospect of reward. Having said that, although it is generally accepted that early-stage funds have a higher than average return vs. later stage ones, many argue this is because early-stage funds take on higher risk, and so from a risk-adjusted point of view, early-stage funds do not necessarily represent a better opportunity.

Seed investors also contribute to the marketability of a fund to other investors, so a fund manager may attempt to get on board an investor with a reputation good enough to encourage investment from others. For example, a commitment to invest from a well-respected FoF will likely encourage other investors to commit as well. The efforts of the pre-launch manager must be focused on investors that have a track record of considering and investing in 'would-be' funds. Furthermore, they must attempt to bring on board investors who, by their very commitment, make the fund more attractive. These 'votes of confidence' from well-respected investors are worth their weight in gold.

Seed investors may, however, demand some extra reward in return for exposing themselves to the risks involved when investing in an unproven fund manager. These rewards may include lowering or waiving the management fees, lowering the performance fees, or part ownership of the management company or some sort of revenue sharing arrangement. If part ownership is agreed, the fund manager is usually granted the right to buy back the seed investor's ownership interest in the management company after a certain period of time, or to pay out higher shares of their revenue or profit for periods of time as a 'buy-out' mechanism. Sometimes such buy outs are enabled only if the fund achieves pre-agreed performance benchmarks. The nature and structure of seed deals vary immensely from one seed investor to the next, and indeed from one deal to the next within a seed investor's portfolio.

Many investors will have a policy of not investing in pre-launch funds. Many FoFs, institutional investors, endowment funds, family and professional offices, and SWFs have strict guidelines that prevent them from investing in any fund before launch, and even during the first 12, 24, or 36 months of operation. Given most funds that cease trading do so in the first year, many investors believe the risks far outweigh the potential upside when investing with early-stage funds.

Note that as per our discussion above, if the fund manager is very well known, his 'new' fund is not strictly speaking a pre-launch fund. Some managers who are starting 'new' funds but have a demonstrable track record, who for example recently shut down their prior fund, may be able to bring with them some of their previous investors as seed investors in their new fund and circumvent minimum 'firm track record length' constraints.

Early Stage

Once a fund has launched, there is a whole new set of investors who become potential targets for a fund. Some investors who are not willing to consider pre-launch, do consider investing within the first year of a fund's existence. In addition to a more extensive number of FoFs and high-net-worth individuals, early-stage funds can focus on certain family and professional offices, and endowment funds. The latter group are very often open to investing in early-stage funds. It is important to note, as we have above, the positive spill-over effects of having certain investors already invested in a fund when attempting to acquire new ones.

This 'positive herd effect' is particularly noticeable during the early stage of a fund. The presence of a well-known FoF in the investor portfolio of an early-stage fund, for example, is a great vote of confidence in the eyes of family and professional offices. If a reputable FoF is invested, they will conclude that the fund has passed a rigorous due diligence and investment rationale examination. FoFs are known to have more stringent and carefully defined due diligence policies, and they usually have a significant investment and diligence team of professionals to appraise each investment opportunity. As some family and professional offices have less manpower, or specific sector expertise, they sometimes rely on previous investor composition as an indicator, or at least a confirmation that the fund in question is robust.

Late Stage

The late stage is, in itself, a pretty good place to be for a start-up hedge fund. Having survived the first full year of operations is a testament to a fund's sustainability. Investors recognize this, and practically no investor will have a lifecycle-based guideline against investing in a late-stage fund. Pension funds, other institutional funds such as banks or insurance funds, and SWFs, will be potential investors to the late-stage fund though for these types of investors they may require a track record longer than a year. That said, at this point, the most risk-adverse investors, with the most stringent guidelines start to become potential investors.

Investor Acquisition – Marketing

We will now discuss the practical aspects of marketing the fund to investors, including choice of marketing channels, potential investor identification, preparation of marketing documentation material, and the marketing cycle. The entire investor acquisition cycle will be discussed, beginning with the successful marketing presentation and expression of interest on the part of the investor to 'continue discussions', followed by the 'site visit', the due diligence process, negotiation of side-letters and related terms, and finally execution and funding of the subscription. 'Know your customer' and related anti-money-laundering practices of different regulatory jurisdictions will be discussed.

Marketing Channels

There are a variety of ways in which funds can raise capital: in-house marketing teams, prime broker capital introduction teams, third-party marketers, and FoFs. We shall review what each option entails, what the typical terms and fees are, and their strengths and weaknesses.

In-house marketing team. A fund may choose to buy or build marketing capabilities in-house, creating a marketing team exclusive to the fund. Having a team focused exclusively on marketing one fund is of course beneficial in that it can count on 100% of the marketing effort. An in-house marketing team will have a deep understanding of the fund, and be able to tailor each investor visit only to the fund it markets. Arranging potential investor meetings with only one fund in mind may allow an in-house marketing team to truly focus its efforts and increase its success ratio. Furthermore, it will be better able to determine and control how the fund is marketed, and ensure the fund is accurately and fairly marketed. With an in-house team, there may be a financial benefit if the cost of developing and retaining own marketing staff is less than the fees prime brokers or consultants would charge.

There are, however, downsides to in-house marketing. First, unless the team has prior experience marketing other funds, or the fund manager has an established record, it is hard for new teams to quickly build up an investor base. Building up an investor base, especially among institutional investors who prefer dealing with those fund managers and marketers they have long-established relationships with, is a time-consuming job. It is therefore probably not the optimum solution for an early-stage fund to invest in in-house capabilities, unless it can market on the back of a fund manager's well-established reputation or it hires a senior enough marketing team that can bring relationships with them.

Second, marketing brings with it some regulatory obligations. In the USA, for example, a fund may have to register as a broker-dealer if it is to market itself, and there are limitations to soliciting investments if a fund wishes to remain exempt from registering under the Securities Act of 1933, and the Investment Company Act of 1940. If a fund wishes not to register with the SEC, solicitation and advertising restrictions may prove to make effective marketing impossible. A US fund may avoid acting as a broker-dealer when employing in-house marketing staff by making use of an issuer exemption, with the condition that its marketing team is not incentivized through compensation linked to their marketing efforts.

Third, a fund manager may get unnecessarily distracted by the in-house marketing team. A fund manager may develop a close working relationship with the in-house team, which becomes a time-consuming distraction that prevents him or her from focusing on investing. Fund managers and in-house teams must work together to minimize the impact of marketing on the fund manager's role as investment manager, keeping the number of investor interactions to a minimum.

Prime brokers. Prime broker firms arose out of the need of asset managers to consolidate their trading, execution, clearing, financing, lending, and cash management services under the roof of a single service provider. Often a division of a global investment bank, prime brokers introduced value-added services into their offering to differentiate themselves, and capital introduction was one of these services. Prime brokers can offer their hedge fund clients introductions to qualified investors they believe will be interested in investing in a particular fund. Prime brokers tend to be more successful in attracting money from their bank's client base, which may include UHNWIs, FoFs, and institutional investors to varying degrees.

It is unusual for prime brokers to charge for their capital introduction services (their revenues are usually derived from financing, trading, and clearing fees), and may therefore be an attractive offering to fund managers. Indeed, there are a number of very capable prime brokerage teams in the market who are very efficient at sourcing capital from their customer base. In addition to being 'free', utilizing a prime broker as a marketer, especially if the prime broker is part of a reputable institution such as a global investment bank, can augment a fund manager's internal marketing efforts.

There are, however, several drawbacks to using prime brokers exclusively as a fund manager's marketers. First, capital introduction being a non-core – and technically a non-fee-generating service – could mean that their capital introduction efforts are not as great as a fund manager would like. For example, many prime brokers organize large conferences for a multitude of funds to meet a select group of investors. It is not unusual for these conferences, however, to not have a significant impact on fundraising efforts. Service providers and other funds usually far outnumber investors, and the generic design of such events often results in investor needs not being matched to investment opportunities. A fund must assess its own value to a prime broker. If a fund is at the smaller end of the spectrum in the portfolio of a given prime broker, or it simply generates less fees (for instance because it does not sell short or leverage its positions very often), a prime broker's capital introduction team may dedicate less of its time and effort to it than the fund requires.

Second, prime brokers may not be as close to the details of the fund as an in-house team or a consultant may be. Prime brokers usually spread their efforts across a large portfolio of funds, and their marketing efforts many times include having investors meet a large number of funds on one day, or organizing conferences for funds to present to investors. Although this breadth of exposure may be beneficial in raising the profile of the fund, it is also likely that this less focused approach will produce a lower success rate and demand a large investment of a fund manager's time that yields little reward.

All things considered, prime brokers can most definitely complement an in-house or consultant-based marketing effort. Given that many prime brokers will offer this service as part of their brokerage package, it would be unwise not to take advantage of it to some extent. Nevertheless, an assessment of how useful prime broker-arranged investor introductions are should be carried out. There comes a point when the opportunity costs of attending investor meeting days or investor conferences will outweigh their benefit. It is crucial to understand how attractive the potential investors introduced by the prime brokerage are, and therefore funds should enquire about them prior to committing to meet them.

Third-party marketers or capital introduction consultants. Companies who specialize in capital introduction for hedge funds are known as third-party marketers (TPMs) or capital introduction consultants. As external providers of marketing services, TPMs are also increasingly involved in helping funds design their strategy or market positioning. We will review that trend of deeper involvement at the end of this section.

TPMs typically negotiate an ongoing participation in the fees generated by the capital they introduce, typically 20% of both management and performance fees (we shall call this the 'participation in fund fees'). Some TPMs only include performance fees in their revenue sharing, and exclude management fees. Others include retainer-based fees, especially if they agree to exclusivity (discussed further below) or to providing dedicated resources. In addition, some also charge an introduction fee on raised capital, especially if it has longer lockups than quarterly redemption cycles. Note that early-stage funds must often agree to higher fees, and sometimes TPMs may demand equity participation in the investment firm as well.

When negotiating an agreement with a TPM, the terms and conditions under which a TPM can claim fees for an investment must be clearly set out. The agreement with a TPM usually covers any affiliates of the fund manager, so if a fund manager controls more than one fund (be it through control of other legal persons or entities), the TPM will be compensated irrespective of whether the investment is made in the fund initially proposed to the investor as an investment opportunity.

TPMs will typically be entitled to compensation for all future investments and incremental investments made by investors introduced to a fund during the term of their agreement. The agreement will cover the eventuality of the fund manager starting up a new fund, whether it is related to the original fund and its entities or not. If investors introduced by a TPM invest again in one of the same fund manager's successive funds, the TPM's claim to its participation in the fund's fees will still apply for an agreed period of time even if the agreement has expired (usually six months to a year). In any case, TPMs will also specify that they are compensated for investments made by investors that were introduced during the agreement term for a period of time after the term of the agreement has expired (usually at least for one year). This provision ensures that TPMs are adequately compensated for having introduced an investor, even if the investor does not make a decision to invest until the TPM agreement has expired.

There are exceptions to these terms. Some TPMs may not demand fund fee participation in perpetuity. They may limit this participation for a fixed period of time, or implement a timeline under which the participation is reduced over time (a 'sunset' or 'waterfall' structure). This is especially the case for TPMs that do not wish to be responsible for an ongoing marketing effort and are simply introducers. An agreement with an all-round TPM should allow room for special introductions by a pure 'introducer' or 'finder' who is not responsible for marketing that fund on an ongoing basis, but who at a given point in time has approached the fund to introduce an investor the main TPM has not identified.

This last exception brings us to an important aspect of TPMs, and that is the extent of their responsibilities versus those of the fund manager with respect to marketing. From the TPM's point of view, we have discussed their role as the ongoing marketer of the fund. They should be in charge of the day-to-day marketing and be proactive in their efforts. Agreements can always be drawn up to include minimum amounts to be raised in set amounts of time with reductions in fees if they are not met. That proactive approach and expectation of delivery (however contractually structured) is the responsibility of the TPM and what differentiates them from more opportunistic 'introducer/finder' TPMs.

The responsibilities of the fund manager vis-à-vis the TPM are numerous. Before any investor has committed to invest, the fund manager must dedicate time and resources to help create marketing materials, attend investor meetings, and answer any questions investors may have. Once invested, the fund manager must also communicate with investors with the regularity and detail that the TPM will have agreed (having pre-agreed it with the fund manager). The fund manager will have to prepare monthly performance reports reviewing recent developments in the market, noteworthy allocation decisions, and fund performance. The fund manager will have to ensure the TPM is kept up to date on any expected or unexpected changes that result in the materials the TPM is using to market the fund becoming obsolete or misleading (e.g., any changes related to the fund manager, or the fund's strategy, performance, legal, compliance, or organizational circumstances). The fund manager will have to provide subscription and redemption data for each investor – for the purpose of calculating the compensation they are due, TPMs require full access to the fund's records (normally through the fund's administrator). As one may expect, fund managers tend to underestimate the time and resources they must dedicate to fulfil their obligations to the TPM. All fund managers should factor these into their plans.

A TPM agreement must allow enough time for the TPM to understand the fund, chart its growth objectives and development plans, carefully design the marketing strategy, prepare the marketing materials, identify appropriate investors, and conduct the marketing process. Fund managers must balance the fixed time commitment of an agreement – and the cost it entails – with the TPM need to spend significant time designing the strategy. If the agreement period is perceived by the TPM to be too short (and the participation in fund fees is somehow limited with regard to the agreement term length), this may incentivize it to bring the fund to market in a hurried fashion, without investing enough time in planning or preparing materials, because it wants to maximize the fees it generates in the agreed time period. Because most agreements allow for TPM participation in fund fees subsequent to agreement term expiry, the TPM concern is in reality more about what the exclusivity situation will become at time of expiry, and this thought process is one the fund manager should follow when negotiating agreement length.

The length of TPM agreements varies, but they are usually not less than a year and more often than not somewhere between two and three. The longer terms will be particularly applicable if the agreement is with a pre-launch or early-stage fund whose appeal to investors is not overwhelming, and therefore does not guarantee a rapid influx of capital in the eyes of the TPM. Fund managers should consider that the longer the term a TPM demands, the more warranted he is to introduce a timeline establishing targets in terms of minimum amounts of assets raised. A fund manager could introduce an automatic termination clause if those targets are not met.

Other than fees, exclusivity is the greatest issue of contention in TPM agreements, and exclusivity is a double-edged sword. TPMs may seek a commitment from the fund that it will not hire another TPM, entity, or individual to raise money for the fund. A fund may also demand the relationship be mutually exclusive, in which case not only does the fund agree to only employ one TPM, but the TPM agrees to not provide its services to any other fund in the same market or product class.

It is important to note that if exclusive, the fund will compensate the TPM for all investors entering the fund. The TPM is compensated irrespective of whether the TPM single-handedly identified the investor and made a successful sale. For example, if an investor contacts the fund directly (having heard about it from another investor), and the fund refers them to the TPM, the TPM still charges its fee.

Having said that, it is common practice to draw up an 'excluded from agreement' investor list prior to a TPM agreement that lists the investors the fund already knows and is in discussions with. The TPM will receive no compensation for investments by any of these excluded investors. Exclusivity simplifies the relationship between the fund and the TPM, and eliminates the grey area around determining whether or not an investor was introduced by the TPM or simply 'convinced' by it.

If the relationship is not exclusive, there should be an agreed method by which the TPM can ring-fence investors at regular intervals. By ring-fencing certain investors, the TPM will specify the names of potential investors that the TPM is proactively marketing the fund to, and for whose investments the TPM will be compensated. A non-exclusive agreement encourages the TPM to include as many investors as possible in their ring-fenced list, to protect their potential compensation. This can lead to a spiral of ring-fencing, especially if there are several TPMs engaged in an agreement with the same fund. The TPMs may end up including almost all potential investors on their individual lists, leading to conflicts between TPMs for ownership of investor relationships.

A similar situation is created if the fund itself ring-fences investors (in essence enlarging the initial list of excluded investors on an ongoing basis). It is reasonable for a fund manager to want to avoid paying fees to the TPM if he is primarily responsible for bringing an investor in as a result of marketing his fund on an ad-hoc basis in parallel with the TPM. However, it is advisable that the fund manager draw up a pre-engagement exclusion list of all the investors he has a relationship with and not subsequently grow this list. This avoids distracting the fund manager from his investing role, avoids arguments with the TPM, and avoids duplication of fundraising efforts. The fund manager should simply refer a potential investor to the fund's TPM.

In general, the competition engendered by non-exclusivity can be counterproductive and difficult to manage. If a fund refers investors to several TPMs that will duplicate efforts, and not necessarily motivate the TPMs to dedicate maximum time to that fund, given that they are facing competition and may lose out on the deal. We feel that exclusivity is preferable to non-exclusivity, and the latter should only be agreed to if carefully planned.

An established portfolio of clients is probably a TPM's most important asset. The more diverse it is in terms of investor types (FoF, pension fund, endowment, etc.) and geographical coverage (pan-European, cross-continental, etc.), the more powerful it will be. The breadth of the investor portfolio will ensure their relevance independent of fund strategy, geographic coverage, or life stage. Some TPMs are particularly focused on a certain investor type, such as family office-focused TPMs, and others are very country focused; for example, covering Switzerland-based clients. Established local relationships and understanding of local investor preference is particularly relevant for transatlantic capital introductions, as investor preferences – even within the same investor type – may vary.

Certain TPMs are sector focused, and within that group some are particularly focused on energy commodities. Funds should attempt to focus their efforts with regard to fundraising, and one of the most efficient ways to minimize time spent on such activities is to involve a niche TPM with sector-specific expertise. They will introduce funds to investors they know have an interest in that particular space. This tailored approach should increase the success ratio of the marketing efforts, and minimize the time spent by fund managers in fundraising meetings. A contrary argument, however, is that by marketing funds which are similar to each other, a TPM may increase the competition between client funds, especially with regard to investors who are only looking to invest in one fund in a given space.

Fund managers should be aware that TPMs not only charge significant fees, and require a significant amount of time, but they also perform detailed appraisals of the funds that may wish to engage them. The due diligence TPMs perform vis-à-vis potential client funds is part of the process through which they collect an understanding about the investment features, operations, and goals of the fund. Fund managers should take into account the investment of time required to go through this due diligence process and minimize its impact on investment activities. Furthermore, fund managers must realize this process is not only to allow the TPM to ensure that a fund is worth representing; they should seize the opportunity to evaluate the quality of the TPM. Funds should assess TPMs around a number of dimensions:

- **Investor base breadth.** A diverse make-up of investors will ensure higher chances of a potential fit. Alternatively, funds may seek out TPMs with an investor base concentration among investors that suit their strategy, sector, or life stage. For example, a pre-launch fund should seek out TPMs with a high concentration of investors interested in seeding opportunities.

- **Geographic coverage.** A broad geographic span is important in that it increases the addressable market. Coverage of either Europe or the USA is of course crucial give the concentration of assets in these two regions. Asian coverage is increasingly important, and more so within the space of energy commodities, a very popular space among Asian investors.

- **Sector/product specialization.** TPMs who specialize in a certain space or strategy may be able to offer higher chances of success given their particular knowledge. In addition to better understanding the funds offering, it should have an investor base with experience and interest in the space.

- **Dedicated resources.** The planned resource and time commitment from a TPM must be sufficient to maximize the chances of success. A fund should inquire into the level of dedicated resources it will receive. Some TPMs have dedicated teams for each account, others are spread thin. Note that if a TPM offers dedicated resources, it may more forcefully argue the need for a retainer to be paid to cover the duration of the engagement.

- **Marketing material quality.** Fund managers should request to see some sample marketing materials prior to working with a TPM. The key to successful marketing is not only performance, but the professionalism, focus, and relevance of its marketing strategy.

- **Image and brand.** Marketers are, at the end of the day, ambassadors for your company. For this reason a fund manager must ensure their chosen TPM projects the image he or she wishes to be associated with.

- **Legal and compliance expertise.** TPMs have particular regulatory obligations given their role in soliciting investments (as discussed, these are particularly stringent in the USA[12]). Fund managers must ensure their TPM has all the necessary regulatory registrations and approvals, and that they are knowledgeable about the developments in financial product marketing legislation in all the geographies in which they operate. In addition, TPMs should be particularly knowledgeable in anti-money-laundering and KYC legislation.

- **Track record.** Fund managers should demand information around a TPM's past achievements. Although not a guarantee of future performance (much like a fund!), a TPM's track record in terms of assets raised should give a fund manager a good indication of their quality, or at least their experience to date.

- **Portfolio of fund clients.** A TPM may not be willing to disclose every one of his clients, but in relation to the question around dedicated resources, it is also important for fund managers to understand which other funds a TPM firm represents. If a TPM represents direct competitors, he may not be able to serve both as well, given the obvious competition between them (in the case of a sector-specialist TPM this is of course an implicit reality).

Teams which help raise funds – be they in-house, prime brokers, FoFs, or TPMs – may also create value beyond purely introducing capital to a fund. This is because they become de facto consultants to the fund manager beyond their asset-raising remit. In addition to capital introduction expertise, high-quality marketers will accumulate expertise regarding how a fund manager can increase the attractiveness of his fund. Marketers understand what investors want, and can be very valuable advisors when it comes to ensuring the positioning, structuring, and strategy of the fund maximizes the addressable market. For example, marketers may advise on particular legal entity designs that make the fund more appealing to certain investors. Fund managers should note that in-house teams with prior experience and TPMs will be the two types of marketers that will add the most value beyond their core competency given that they will (usually) have more in-depth knowledge of the fund and potential investors (e.g., compared to a prime broker or a FoF).

---

[12]In the USA, TPMs sell shares in a fund and charge for it, this usually means they must be licensed as a registered representative of a broker-dealer.

Fund of funds as marketing channels. FoFs offer diversification across many individual funds, and their offering is simply the sum of its parts: the underlying funds. By accepting FoFs as investors, funds effectively allow FoFs to serve as indirect marketers for them. The degree to which this marketing is explicit varies from one FoF to another. Some FoFs will not disclose which funds make up their portfolio, whilst others are very open about particular relationships. Large FoFs are increasingly associated with large institutional investors, who demand a more transparent relationship and a higher degree of disclosure around investment allocations. FoFs at the more transparent end of the spectrum will typically reveal details such as which funds they have the largest holdings in (if not all), what percentage of their fund each of those holdings represents, or what their stakeholding is in each of the underlying funds. Another reason why some FoFs market underlying funds more explicitly is that FoFs become more closely associated with funds they have made an early-stage investment in. Many funds grant FoFs preferential investment terms if they are an early investor, and one of these perks may be a capacity reservation. Under such an agreement, the FoF has the right to invest an agreed amount of further capital in an agreed time frame (or a percentage of new capacity created).

FoFs therefore present their capacity reservation agreements with funds that are otherwise closed as part of their value proposition to investors. Furthermore, FoFs may associate themselves with particularly renowned and over-performing funds in order to raise their own profile and underline their discerning investment decisions.

Word of mouth. Although not an easily controllable marketing channel, word of mouth plays an important part in generating introductions for a marketing team. Although it should not be relied on to generate leads, fund managers should be aware that word of mouth can be a source of investors, and they will find themselves referring investors who contact them directly to their marketing team (be it in-house or not). Word of mouth is more effective in generating FoF and UHNWI leads who talk more among themselves and interact more with the market. Institutional investors like pension funds, endowments, and SWFs are less social creatures that rely less on word of mouth and will therefore require targeted approaches.

Pre-launch and early-stage funds will usually be unable to afford setting up an in-house marketing team, especially if they want that team to bring experience and contacts with them. Some funds may be able to afford building in-house capabilities, but will realize – after a relatively brief analysis – that investing the budget in bolstering their analytical and trading capabilities will increase their value-generating capacity to such an extent that it outweighs the potential savings to be had by cutting fundraising costs.

Money is far better spent by start-up funds on research, analysis, and trading capacity than it is on building or buying marketing expertise.

Prime broker capital introduction services are an avenue worth exploring, but must be used wisely or they will take up a lot of a fund manager's time. In addition, they may not be as focused or knowledgeable as is necessary given their broader remit and the ancillary nature of their existence. TPMs are probably the best option in that they bring with them experience and their own database of potential investors. Many institutional investors in particular are more easily accessible through TPMs who have established relationships with them. TPMs can also add value by advising on ways to make the fund more attractive, and give input on fund strategy design with regard to its predictable impact on the marketability of the fund.

Tools for Marketing and Key Marketing Documents

Although building marketing capabilities up-front may not be the wisest decision for an early-stage fund, it is worth understanding what the main marketing tools are, and what the important features of the key marketing documents are.

Investor databases. When it comes to building up a database with details of investors you can approach, the quickest way is to purchase investor contact details from firms that specialize in amassing this information. Providers of investor databases offer a variety of products. In addition to simple contact details, providers also offer profile information about investors including their management, disposable assets, assets invested, current asset allocation estimates, previous known allocations, current allocation strategy and priorities, and preferred products, strategies, and markets. The quality of investor databases varies widely, and if considering buying one, a fund manager should only consider purchasing one from the reputable players in the market. Given that the quality of these databases is difficult to verify – beyond the basic contact details – there is a high incidence of low-quality providers.

One of the main determinants of its quality and usefulness is how up-to-date the database is. In a fast-moving environment like asset allocation, contact details will not necessarily change often, but the preferences, strategies, and plans will, making out-of-date information almost useless. Fund managers must take a view on how they will use the database when deciding between a one-off purchase or a subscription service. If a quick initial base to start on is required, to later be complemented by research on the phone and online, perhaps a subscription is not required. If the database is to form most of the foundation research for reaching out to investors for the foreseeable future, maybe a subscription service is a worthwhile budget commitment. In both cases, enquiring about the regularity with which the data is updated will be very important, and more specifically, what percentage of the database is updated every time, on average.

To understand whether or not a database will suit your needs, and to assess its quality, all reputable providers should give a sample upon request. It is very important to make sure that the data fields included, the format in which it is presented, and the ease with which it can be manipulated all meet expectations. Prices range from USD 500 to USD 5000 for most one-off purchases, with monthly updated subscription services costing from USD 200 a month up to USD 20,000 a year.

Hedge fund databases. As well as investor databases that enable funds to target potential investors, there is a market for hedge fund databases that enable investors to map out the investment opportunities available to them. Including your own fund on a hedge fund database is also helpful in generating investor interest and raising the profile of your fund. In fact, some investors go as far as only considering the funds on the proprietary databases of their investment advisors, especially institutional investors.

If you do decide to make information about your fund available on commercial databases, it is important to include all the relevant information and to maintain it up-to-date. In addition to top-level strategy information, it is helpful to include data around the fund characteristics such as: AUM, domicile, currency denomination, and main service providers.

Industry publications and electronic communication platforms. Over the last 10 to 15 years, a large body of hedge fund industry-specific publications has emerged. There are numerous magazines, electronic news subscription services, websites, and online networking groups dedicated to the world of hedge funds. Furthermore, there are focused publications catering to pretty much every geographic market, investment style, and industry.

These publications can be useful to both track investor activity and publicize one's own fund. Noteworthy events such as launching a new fund, expanding into new markets, or hiring a new trader are good reasons to contact these publications and provide them with relevant information to publish. Additionally, some publications (e.g., EuroHedge) also list funds and may include performance figures.

Conferences. Hedge fund conferences represent a useful networking forum for funds and investors alike. Before discussing their key attributes, it is worth mentioning that the perceived usefulness of conferences varies significantly depending on whom you ask. Conferences are purely social events to some and genuinely useful business-making opportunities to others. How useful a conference is to market your fund will of course depend on the nature and quality of the conference, but also on how you approach it.

Most conferences will feature a series of speakers – usually a variety of investors, fund managers, FoF managers, and service providers. Some conferences will also feature investor 'roundtables' where managers and investors meet to discuss potential investments. These roundtables may be arranged on an ad-hoc basis, or they may be planned and agreed in advance if the conference organizer circulates the attendee list and coordinates the prior set-up of the meeting. A special version of the former that has proved quite popular at conferences we have attended is the hedge fund world equivalent of speed dating. Under this ad-hoc meeting format, attendees do not even have to strike up a conversation with another party and sit down to meet – the meetings are set up so that all managers have a short amount of time to meet each investor, and they rotate around, 'speed dating' style. Although perhaps not incredibly targeted, it does increase the number of investors each manager comes in contact with.

All conferences will also make time for more informal networking opportunities, usually over a few drinks. One particularly memorable conference organized a rock concert featuring The Who, however this is not the norm.

Attending conferences can quickly become a very costly affair, in terms of both time and money. Unless one manages to be invited as an official speaker, in which case the attendance fees are waived (though no fee is usually paid), most conferences will have a registration fee of at least USD 1000. Large multi-day conference registration fees may range from USD 5000 to USD 10,000, especially if an 'exhibit booth' is included. On top of registration fees, all hotel and travel expenses will have to be covered by the fund, and usually the chosen locations and hotels are at the expensive end of the spectrum.

If carefully selected, conferences can be very helpful to build up contacts quickly. Conferences are particularly helpful for early-stage funds which need to amass as many investor contacts as possible, as quickly as possible. Before registering for any given conference, the fund manager should be sure to request a list of attendants and evaluate whether the conference has a sufficient percentage of investors, and whether these investors are ones he does not yet have a relationship with. It is also helpful to use the attendee list to base one's own research on, seeking out their contact details and any interesting information on the Internet. If a large number of investors are attending whom the fund has never met, and the cost of registration, accommodation, travel, and manager time are reasonable, the conference may well be an effective and rapid way to build up an investor portfolio and increase visibility in the market.

When attending conferences, it is ideal to combine the forces of the fund manager with those of whoever is responsible for in-house marketing (or the TPM representative, if there is one). The investors will be most interested in meeting the fund manager, who will in turn be able to answer the more sophisticated questions. Ideally, the marketer will coach the fund manager on the profile of each investor, and tailor the sales pitch (both his own and that of the fund manager) to the preferences of each.

Though different in structure then the conferences described above, prime brokers also host different conferences or manager events where a prime broker invites a group of promising fund managers and a number of potential investors to meet the managers. These types of conferences are usually organized by some sort of theme, usually geography (e.g., Asian manager conference for investors interested in managers focused on Asia). During the course of the event, a manager will generally meet with a number of different potential investors at time during meetings throughout the day and be able to present their story and answer any questions investors may have.

Marketing Documentation

The marketing documents of a fund are very often the medium through which first impressions are made to an investor. Even if introductory meetings are arranged, marketing documents will always be circulated in advance. This means the documents used to market the fund are of paramount importance. They must transmit a sense of professionalism and serious business acumen. The main documents are:

- the monthly performance report
- the 'road-show' marketing presentation.

The offering memorandum and the due diligence questionnaire (DDQ, please see Appendix C) also play an important role in marketing a fund, even though they are not technically regarded as marketing documents. We discuss their roles in greater detail in Chapters 6 and 10 and in the relevant Appendix.

The Monthly Performance Report

The monthly performance report is a brief report covering the main features of the fund, updated monthly with performance data and commentary around relevant market developments. Given that there is little performance to report pre-launch, this report is in the realm of early- or late-stage funds.

Before trading begins, however, some start-up fund managers might consider writing a market commentary that will obviously not include performance (as nothing has been traded yet) but will include a fund manager's view on the market.

Once trading begins and performance can be reported, a fund manager will write a report also known as a monthly letter, monthly report, or in some variants a 'teaser'. The latter term alludes to its function as a tool to entice investors to investigate the fund further. This is because not only do investors currently invested in the fund receive the performance report as a monthly update on how the fund is performing, but prospective investors are sent it too in order to encourage investment. One could argue that the main objective of this latter style of report is to sell rather than inform. Some funds will have longer in-depth monthly reports to current investors and shorter teaser versions for prospects. Prospective investors who are not yet interested enough to participate in an initial marketing meeting, or perform a due diligence visit, will be sent this latter format of the report as a way of ensuring the fund remains on the radar screen, and ultimately warrants a closer look.

Like all good selling materials, the monthly performance report must tell a compelling story. It must be well designed, with a clear layout making it attractive to read. In addition, it must be as informative as possible, answering the potential questions investors will have when reading it. When trying to design the content to pre-empt potential questions, a fund may consider tailoring their monthly performance report differently depending on whether the recipient is a current or a prospective investor. Current investors will be more interested in the performance, and the market and portfolio commentary. The version for prospective investors should be weighted more towards pointing out the fund's unique competitive advantage. Larger funds may afford the time and resources required to tailor the monthly performance report even further, based on group or even individual hot-buttons. Naturally, the more targeted the materials, the more effective they will prove to be.

To create a compelling story, the document should highlight the strengths of the fund, describing its competitive advantage, what sets it apart from other funds. An effective monthly performance report will contain the following information.

1. **Intuitively displayed return performance data.** Performance is what investors seek and the first thing they will want to see. This applies to both current and prospective investors. Return performance figures should be displayed by month for the full lifetime of the fund. It is also standard practice to include the returns calculated in terms of year to date, inception to date, and compound annual return. To ensure correctness (or at

least decrease liability for possible errors), fund managers should utilize administrator calculated and approved figures as well as send investor weekly internal estimates via email. Fund managers should note that performance data should always reflect the returns under standard investment terms. This implies that existing investors who have negotiated specific investment terms (lower performance fees, for example) may find the report informative overall but less useful in terms of absolute figures reported.

2. **Insightful and widely used performance metrics.** In addition to straightforward return measures, investors will expect to find a number of standard statistical measurements around performance and volatility. Although there are a myriad of statistics to choose from, the two most commonly used are standard deviation and Sharpe ratio. Standard deviation measures the variation of a fund's return over a set period of time. In essence it shows the extent to which a fund's returns are consistent to its mean return, and hence 'predictable'. It is common practice to show annualized standard deviation (i.e., volatility) and to do so for every relevant time period (annual or year to date).

The Sharpe ratio has become an industry standard measure for risk-adjusted fund performance and all investors will expect to find it on the monthly performance report. It was originally devised to measure the rate of return generated by a fund relative to the amount of risk taken to achieve the return (i.e., rate of return generated per unit of risk). This ratio measures the rate of return above a minimum risk-free rate, because a low rate of return is always achievable by taking no risk. The Sharpe ratio is hence calculated as the average excess return divided by the volatility of excess returns. The higher the excess return or the lower the volatility, the higher the ratio and the better performing the fund manager is thought to be – because he has provided the most return relative to the risk he took. Having said that, the issue with this ratio is that it employs volatility as a measure of risk, and volatility is not necessarily representative of risk. It is a fair proxy in some cases, but a poor one in most. Risks will have been taken to achieve a certain rate of return, which will not be reflected in the volatility. With that caveat in mind, funds can argue that when comparing funds within the same space, and with similar strategies, the non-captured risk may affect the compared funds similarly and to some extent cancel out.

To show risk, some funds use what has become commonly referred to as the Sortino ratio. One could argue that this ratio is a more 'helpful' alternative to standard deviation, given that standard deviation takes all deviations into account equally, i.e., large positive surprises lead to higher volatility although usually no investor would complain about this. What investors usually worry about are large deviations of returns to the downside and Sortino and other ratios try to address this by looking specifically at only the negative side of the return distribution rather than all return realizations. To illustrate this, consider a fund that delivers consistently negative returns of –3% to –4% a month. It will have a very low standard deviation but that does not make it a fund worth investing in. Conversely, a fund with relatively volatile positive returns could arguably be said to be 'penalized' with a high standard deviation even though its volatility is 'good'. The Sortino ratio intends to only capture negative deviation. Rather than measuring volatility across the universe of potential returns, it limits its measurement of volatility to downside deviations below a set level of return. Detractors of this measurement would argue that this understates the risks taken to achieve the positive returns but which did not negatively impact them. Note that when ignoring a part of the realized return distribution an investor would chose to ignore data with additional informational content. As many hedge funds only report monthly returns, cutting-off data points from the analysis may lead to a situation where results are no longer statistically significant. For instance, in order to calculate a meaningful number for standard deviation at least 30 data points are needed (i.e., 2.5 years of monthly data). Assuming that 50% of months are positive, however, by cutting-off positive realizations this would now require 5 years of track-record. This issue can solved if more frequent returns are made accessible.

There are strategic decisions to be made with regard to which statistics should be featured on the monthly performance report. Although the measures discussed above will be expected, and raise eyebrows if absent, there are many ways to tailor the selection of metrics to tell a story as compellingly as possible. For example, if there was a change that improved performance considerably – a shift in strategy, a new trader, new risk management processes, or increased geographic coverage – it may be useful to define a time period commencing at the time of the change, effectively segmenting the fund performance into a 'before' and 'after' time period. Defining the reference time period to one's advantage can also be achieved by using rolling return data, to emphasize performance since inception and not be bound by calendar years. A final example would be the treatment of a high standard deviation resulting from positive volatility. As an alternative, the Sortino ratio could be used to display a 'better' ratio. Although performance 'is what it is', strategically chosen performance metrics will help turn a fund's performance into a compelling story. The objective of the monthly performance report is to both retain current investors and attract prospective ones. With respect to the latter objective, all the report must achieve is to prompt a more in-depth due diligence process and hence the information displayed must not be complete, simply sufficient.

3. **Relevant performance benchmarks.** Investors will appreciate it if the monthly performance report does the grunt work in terms of providing them with the necessary comparative analysis and data. Investors will of course perform their own comparisons, but the power of comparative analysis showing your fund outperforming the competition is a very compelling selling tool. In addition to standalone performance metrics, relative metrics highlighting the performance of a fund relative to its peers (i.e., funds with a similar strategy and trading in the same space) could be very powerful – assuming the comparison is favourable of course.

   The benchmarks must be chosen to ensure the most relevant comparison, whilst also showing the most favourable comparison possible. This trade-off between relevance and convenience is not always an easy ask to resolve, given that investors will assume the comparison was not particularly flattering to the fund if it did not include a standard benchmark. Strategic selection, however, is again important, just as it is in choosing performance metrics. Although comparative analyses are usually focused on performance, volatility benchmarking can be useful as well. For example, a fund aiming for low returns and low volatility relative to its peers may seem unattractive from a pure return perspective. Benchmarked in volatility terms, however, it may satisfy the return profile of an investor looking for a lower-return/lower-volatility investment. Remember, a fund must always make sure to obtain approval to include these benchmarks if such approval is necessary.

4. **Market and portfolio commentary.** Current and prospective investors alike will pay particular attention to commentary around recent developments in the market, and changes in the fund's portfolio allocation. Commentary plays an explanatory role, building on the numerical data and explaining the drivers behind the figures. It should be used to explain both negative and positive trends, and give a feeling for future market opportunity. It will usually be written by the fund manager, with input from his team, and should include topics such as:

   - recent and future market developments;
   - recent fund performance relative to the market, and the drivers behind it;
   - the drivers behind any major performance or volatility swings (positive and negative);

- a high-level commentary on major trades (profitable or otherwise);
- typical portfolio allocation and any recent changes in its composition.

The primary concern of fund managers in composing the market commentary, and describing the portfolio allocation, will be not revealing too much. It must be assumed that although these reports are sent out as confidential and proprietary documents only intended for the use of the recipient, they will be disseminated further to third parties. Fund managers must be secretive about their trading approach for obvious reasons, but they must also be informative and insightful enough in their updates to create a rapport with existing investors, and allow potential investors to build an accurate picture of the investment opportunity. Fund managers will typically reveal certain positions only once they have been exited, and only indicate portfolio composition at a high level (by product or geography). Funds will find that depending on the lifecycle, the degree of transparency must be tailored. Very young funds, for example, may have to reveal more detailed information to attract investors, whereas established ones can get away with being less informative. With both existing and prospective investors, but particularly with the former, monthly or quarterly updates in the form of face-to-face meetings or conference calls will supplement the market and portfolio commentary. It is safer for funds to go into more detail in conversation, and in doing so they can also tailor their transparency to the needs and preferences of each investor, only revealing what is required.

5. **Key investment information.** Presenting an overview of the key investment information in one easy reference document is very helpful to investors. For some fund managers, this might be a term sheet or a page in a presentation that represents information that might be found in a term sheet. A good marketing document should make it easy for investors to find the information they seek, and providing a summary of the key fund information investors are certain to want to know is crucial. Although particularly helpful to prospective investors, existing investors will also appreciate the reminder, saving them the work of having to review the offering documents to find relevant information. Standard key information covers the following.

   - *Fund structure detail and entities:* fund domicile, investment manager, investment advisor, fund manager.
   - *Investment terms:* management fee, performance fee, subscription dates and terms, minimum initial subscription size, subsequent subscription size, redemption dates and terms (e.g., redemption fees and redemption gate).
   - *Service providers:* administrator, custodian, auditor, legal counsel, clearing house.

- *Investor relations contact data:* primary contact of the in-house marketing team or details of the TPM.

6. **Competitive advantage overview.** A fund should endeavour to catalogue its unique strengths to increase its appeal. These may cover aspects such as the fund manager's stellar reputation, the power of their analytical team and modelling resources, proprietary information-gathering capabilities, etc. The competitive advantage overview should briefly and succinctly highlight what makes a fund unique, what its 'edge' is. This section will be particularly important if the report recipients are prospective investors. As discussed, the monthly performance report should ideally be tailored to both groups, and this section should be more prominent and lengthy in the case of a prospective investor audience.

The performance report should be brief. Depending on the level of detail, number of visuals, and age of the fund, the report should be anywhere between one and four pages long. Longer reports tend to be ineffective due to a lack of focus and excess detail. Although using standard word-processing software could be sufficient, the use of publishing software will ensure a more crisp and professional look and feel, particularly with regard to the layout and visuals. It is important to design the template so that it can be updated in a time-efficient manner. Investing up-front in the design and underlying models necessary to generate the performance metrics will ensure that the time required for monthly updating is minimized.

A final consideration around the monthly performance report is the format of communication. There are a number of delivery media available, and a fund should endeavour not only to have it available in all media but also to ensure the medium utilized matches the preferences of each investor. The most common form of communication is via e-mail, usually as an attached PDF to ensure the formatting is consistent. Some investors will also want it sent to them in hard copy, and others will prefer to access it online in a virtual data room set up for this purpose.

The Marketing Presentation

The marketing presentation is a document designed to give an overview of a fund, featuring information very similar to that covered in the monthly performance report. This presentation can also be designed to include all the monthly performance report information, excluding performance data, for the purposes of marketing a fund that has not yet launched. Pre-launch funds should treat their marketing presentation as the main marketing document up until launch, and prepare the monthly performance report prior to launch to ensure it is ready to go by the end of the first month of operation.

For pre-launch funds, the marketing presentation will be the main document sent to investors to elicit pre-launch investments. It will be the basis for their initial 'selling' interaction, usually sent prior to a face-to-face meeting or initial due diligence site visit.

For funds already in operation, the presentation may be sent to prospective investors as an initial selling interaction, and then complemented with the monthly performance report or 'teaser'. Or it may be sent after the teaser as a way of elaborating on the information contained therein. The marketing team must make a call on whether the investor prefers brief concise information first, followed by a more in-depth treatment, or vice-versa.

A marketing presentation is usually written in slide format (using software such as Microsoft PowerPoint), and covers the same topics as the monthly performance report. It does, however, go into slightly more detail, and is more structured in its storyboard. A typical marketing presentation would be structured in the following manner (this example is for a fund that is already operating, the only difference from a pre-launch presentation being that the information is actual rather than planned).

1. **Legal disclaimer.** Legal language establishing the document as confidential and proprietary, clarifying the document complies with local regulation in terms of its function as material marketing financial investments, and reminding investors of the inherent risk of investing in investment funds.

2. **Fund overview.** Covering high-level strategy and coverage, launch date, and any major information about the fund itself.

3. **Organizational structure.** A detailed mapping out of the legal entities that make up the fund, explaining the ownership structure. A clear diagram is usually helpful.

4. **Objectives of the fund.** High-level summary of the return and volatility targets, main traded products and geographies, maximum capacity, and any other relevant targets of the fund such as non-correlation to equities or low leverage.

5. **Team overview.** Profile of the fund manager, main trader(s), and/or risk manager underlining previous experience and track record.

6. **Competitive advantage.** Overview of any distinguishing factors that give the fund an edge over the competition (analytical power, proprietary research, dedicated risk management team, etc.).

7. **Investment environment.** Background including market size, market dynamics, product universe, drivers of profitable opportunities, competitive environment, recent and future market and regulatory developments, major

market trends, and future market outlook. Depending on how sophisticated the audience is, funds must tailor this to educate the audience to a greater or lesser degree. Energy commodity markets are relatively new to most investors and not as ubiquitous as equity markets, for example, hence funds should err on the side of explaining too much rather than too little.

8. **Target portfolio allocation/typical positions and strategies.** Breakdown of target portfolio by product (e.g., power vs. emissions), instrument (e.g., exchange cleared vs. OTC), or geographic market (e.g., Germany vs. Norway); indicative strategy weighting (e.g., directional vs. relative value).

9. **Future plans.** Overview of what the short- and medium-term plans are in terms of: AUM, additional intellectual capital, product or geographic coverage, return or volatility objectives, exchange memberships, etc.

10. **Performance metrics.** Return data; performance metrics such as standard deviation and Sharpe ratio; comparative benchmarks.

11. **Investment terms.** List of fund entities such as the fund domicile, investment manager, investment advisor, fund manager; investment terms such as the management fee, performance fee, subscription dates and terms, minimum initial and subsequent subscription, redemption dates and terms (redemption fees and gate); list of service providers such as the administrator, cash custodian, auditor, legal counsel, clearing house.

12. **Contact information.** Contact details of the primary contact of the in-house marketing team or details of the TPM.

Final Remarks

Even though performance is a requisite for attracting investors, it is not sufficient. The image of professionalism created by the marketing materials that attempt to present this performance in the most appealing and relevant way will be an immediate proxy for the professionalism of the trading operation. Even if only subconsciously, investors will judge the merits of the fund on the merits of its communication materials. They are usually the first reference point and interaction between a fund and an investor, and it is up to them to enable a second round of due diligence. It is critical to get beyond the first stage of contact, and achieving this is normally entirely up to the marketing documents. Funds must invest considerable time up-front and in the continuous updating and refinement of these materials. They lie at the heart of a successful investor acquisition.

One final note on data and information integrity. The importance of ensuring these figures are correctly calculated cannot be overemphasized. Not only do errors destroy credibility, they may lead to regulatory intervention or litigation if they are interpreted to be purposefully misleading or fraudulent. Accordingly, it generally makes sense to provide data to investors and potential investors in order for them to conduct their own analyses.

Investor Maintenance – Investor Relations

Many fund managers seem to be somewhat shy or reticent when it comes to communicating with investors. Even though a great deal of effort is made during the acquisition stage of the marketing cycle, both interest and effort vanish once capital is secured. Learning to understand and work with investors past a successful acquisition stage is, however, one of the most important long-term success factors for a fund manager and his fund.

Different investors require different forms and frequency of communication. Investors with clearly institutionalized reporting processes will demand more formal interactions with clearly defined regularity. Furthermore, they will specify their minimum expectations in terms of transparency. Existing investors can reasonably demand monthly updates, in the form of the monthly performance report. They can also expect live conference call updates, with the participation of the fund manager, at least once a quarter.

Some investors will present the fund with their own template of required information and expect the fund to complete it on a monthly or quarterly basis. Such information request templates usually include fields such as: AUM, number of investors, number of active positions or strategy plays, allocation to different markets and products, recent changes in intellectual capital personnel.

The need to respond to ad-hoc enquiries is a frequently underestimated time commitment. Such ad-hoc demands can be of many kinds, but are usually related to questions that may arise related to recent events, market rumours, or legal and regulatory clarifications around the fund structure or set-up that may be relevant to the investor's own legal team. Preparation should be made for in-house staff to dedicate time to this purpose.

The provisions above are based on standard expectations under standard circumstances. Funds must, however, be aware of the difference between routine communications and communications during stressful situations such as periods of poor performance. It is in cases of extraordinary circumstances – be they fund specific or market related – that communication becomes even more critical in maintaining investor confidence. An unnecessary atmosphere of secrecy is often created at the beginning of the relationship between funds and investors. This lack of transparency and openness often translates into an unnecessary climate of mistrust later on in the relationship, often triggered by periods of disappointing performance. Maintaining the appropriate level of transparency and clarity in every communication throughout the relationship often lowers redemption risk during challenging periods. This means that information released to any given investor from day one should always be made available. If the level of information is varied, it should always be to include more and not less. The latter causes suspicion that something may be awry. Of course it is possible to have differentiated transparency in the sense of having early-stage investors be privy to more information than later-stage ones. But again this must be carefully managed, both from a regulatory and a reputational point of view. A fund does not want to be legally liable for unequal treatment of investors, and it does not want to create a reputation of favouring some investors over others.

Early-stage funds, given their lack of track record, will have to be more flexible in their availability for updates, and perhaps more open about their current trading strategy and positions. Like in any business, with a position of strength (in the fund world an enviable track record and established reputation) comes the ability to set one's own rules and decrease flexibility and responsiveness to the demands of others.

On an investor-by-investor level, the following high-level generalizations may be helpful.

1. **Sovereign wealth funds.** Sovereign wealth funds will have clearly established update regularity requirements, usually monthly. Depending on the level of transparency they demand (oftentimes a function of the transparency they impose on themselves), they may expect a high degree of disclosure. To some extent, given the public nature of these institutions, there is a belief that confidential information has a higher chance of remaining so than among private players.

2. **Fund of hedge funds.** FoFs have their own reporting cycles and updates, usually monthly, and will surely demand and expect monthly and even bi-monthly updates. There is some degree of discomfort among funds with the level of FoFs' disclosure, because FoFs have their own clients and are invested in a large range of funds, often in the same space. The degree to which sensitive information stays within the company is sometimes questioned. Funds should make sure they underline the

confidential nature of their updates, and make themselves comfortable with the discretion of their FoF investors.

3. **Endowment funds.** Endowment funds are usually highly institutionalized and will have clearly established update regularity requirements, usually monthly.

4. **Pension and insurance funds.** Pension and insurance funds are usually highly institutionalized and demand a high level of transparency. Given the degree of scrutiny most pension funds are subject to, they will have clearly established update regularity requirements, usually monthly, and clearly defined information requirements.

5. **Family office funds.** Large family offices are usually highly institutionalized and demand a high level of transparency. They will have clearly established update regularity requirements, and given their more long-term investment style, these tend to include high-level monthly updates and more detailed quarterly updates. They are more flexible and vague in terms of their information requirements.

6. **Professional office funds.** Professional office funds will have clearly established update regularity requirements, and given their more long-term investment style, these tend to include high-level monthly updates and more detailed quarterly updates. They are more flexible and vague in terms of their information requirements.

7. **UHNWIs.** UHNWIs tend to require more sporadic updates, but may require them out of cycle at short notice if they suddenly decide to make adjustments to their portfolio. Their behaviour is less predictable than that of large organizations, and the spectrum of transparency requirements varies significantly.

8. **Retail customers.** Retail customer aggregators will have clearly established update regularity and transparency requirements. Given the degree of scrutiny, institutions that provide retail customers with access to hedge funds will have clearly established update regularity requirements, usually monthly, and clearly defined information requirements.

Chapter 9

Operations and Infrastructure

I'm not into this detail stuff. I'm more concepty.
Donald H. Rumsfeld, former US Secretary of Defense

Introduction

If your approach to operations and infrastructure functions echoes the excerpted statement made by the former US Secretary of Defense, then things do not bode well for your hedge fund endeavour. Generally, clients invest in alternative investments, such as hedge funds, for superior risk-adjusted returns that offer capital protection and capital appreciation. Clients expect hedge funds and other investment firms to achieve this goal through consistency. Sophisticated clients want to see evidence of consistency in the investment process, risk management, operations, and across other core functions from any investment manager.

During a meeting, we once heard a highly regarded trader mention a key tenet of managing a successful investment enterprise. He said something to the effect of: 'You can be the best trader in the world but if you don't have a good operations staff, then it doesn't matter.' We wholeheartedly agree with his statement. Accordingly, this chapter is about the key concepts we have found essential for ensuring that operations and other back-office functions contribute to the overall success of the investment management enterprise.

As different hedge funds will undoubtedly have different operational needs depending on investment style, asset class, use of derivatives, frequency of trading, jurisdictions and geographies that a hedge fund may transact, and a host of other factors, we have focused on core principles that should be relevant to hedge fund managers irrespective of trading strategy or geography. In our experience, there are four core principles that should be kept in mind as one builds out operations and other back-office functions. We broadly refer to these as the 'infrastructure', and include areas such as compliance and technology. The four core principles that a successful hedge fund needs to get right are:

1. risk
2. people
3. processes
4. procedures.

Risk

To properly create a suitable operational framework, a hedge fund needs to have a proper understanding of the total risk that needs to be managed, which begins with market risk but includes operational risk, regulatory risk, and other similar risk factors. Accordingly, operations are a core part of a hedge fund's risk management function and will likely encompass – at the minimum – trade processing and reconciliation as well as portfolio valuation. Though an administrator will be calculating the official monthly net asset value of the fund, the firm's staff will need to confirm that the administrator is performing its duties correctly. Additionally, operations teams will likely be engaged in ever-increasing regulatory reporting and portfolio monitoring functions to ensure the holdings of the investment portfolio are consistent with the rules and laws for the relevant markets that a hedge fund may be trading.

Ultimately, there is nothing worse than losing investment gains through poor operational procedures and back-office failures. In order to avoid such issues we feel that besides risk, the other three core principles to focus on are people, processes, and procedures, or what we uncreatively refer to as 'the three Ps'. Though unoriginal in name, the three Ps form the pillars of any robust operational framework.

People

Beyond the founding investment professionals, for most start-up hedge funds the next partner or employee that will be hired is often a chief operations officer (COO), operations manager, or equivalent role. Depending on the needs of the hedge fund and the background of the founder(s), the background of this hire could vary. For some hedge funds, it may make sense for the COO to be a person with a finance or accounting background and to serve a dual COO/chief financial officer (CFO) function. For other firms, it may make sense to bring on someone that has deep operations experience gained at another investment firm or an investment bank. For firms that have greater legal or regulatory requirements due to their investment style or the jurisdictions in which they operate, perhaps it might make sense for the COO to be a lawyer and serve a dual COO/legal and/or compliance officer role. Increasingly, this latter function is taking up a lot of management time given the rise in regulatory demands from jurisdictions across the world, including the USA and Europe. Young funds may not be able to afford a separate COO and compliance officer, so a person with a compliance background or disposition in a lead operational role can be very helpful.

Irrespective of who is hired, the first step before taking resumes and screening candidates is to think critically about what skills and experiences are needed for the COO in order for the firm to be successful. The needs of a hedge fund may change over its lifecycle, going from start-up to more established, so ideally the firm should hire an operations professional who is able to contribute to the firm through these stages.

Once a professional is hired to lead operations for the hedge fund then at some point an operations team will likely need to be hired. That team could be just one other professional besides the COO or a larger team as assets under management grow. Each start-up hedge fund will be different, but there are two main schools of thought about hiring. On the one hand, particularly when financial resources are scarce, a firm may hire on an as-needed basis. For example, as operational intensity increases then a firm may look to hire additional employees to lessen the burden on its existing team. The downside of this strategy is that it takes time and energy to identify the right candidate. Even if the screening, interviewing, and hiring process is relatively quick for a particular hire, it will still take a number of months for that new hire to be functional and trained to satisfy the requirements of the role. So it may end up being six months to a year for that new hire to fully contribute to the team.

Conversely, firms can hire on prospective need. This approach makes sense if a hedge fund is not constrained financially and/or has reasonably high confidence that they will be able to raise capital fairly quickly in the foreseeable future. By hiring on prospective need, ideally new staff are already trained up when the operational intensity increases, thus minimizing growing pains as the firm matures. Obviously, a downside of this approach is if – for whatever reason – operational intensity does not increase and the firm now has unnecessary headcount cost. These types of hiring decisions are emblematic of the broader planning that a hedge fund founder needs to prudently undertake in order to successfully manage the business side (i.e., non-portfolio management aspect) of a hedge fund.

Processes

The *sine qua non* to ensure a successful operations function for any financial services firm, including a hedge fund, is having correct and consistent processes. As investors in hedge funds like to see a consistent investment process that is repeatable, this principle applies equally for operations. In the current fundraising environment, hedge fund investors not only want to see excellent performance, they also want to see evidence that a hedge fund has strong operations and infrastructure. For start-up hedge funds that aspire to be institutional quality asset managers, performance is only one side of the coin. The other side of the coin is robust operations and infrastructure, which institutional investors are evaluating with increasing scrutiny. The key to this is logical, repeatable operational processes that are not overly reliant on manual work, calculations, and human interventions, which ultimately increase the likelihood of human error. Furthermore, these processes should be characterized by a high degree of checks and balances and built-in redundancies in order to minimize mistakes that could result from both human error and automated processes.

Procedures

Once quality processes have been established they need to be documented. We refer to these documented processes as procedures. Procedures are helpful for a few different reasons. Once processes have been documented as procedures then they are easily repeatable. Procedures also make it easy to make diagnoses and corrections when there are operational errors. Occasionally, these procedures will be helpful when dealing with regulators and prospective investors who may want a better understanding of various operational processes. Finally, by creating procedures it helps institutionalize knowledge. For example, when an employee departs not all of the functional knowledge related to the role will be taken if there are clear and complete procedures. Similarly, when a new employee joins the firm it will be easier to train and acclimatize them if there are easy-to-reference procedures.

Generally, these procedures need to outline: a) what the process is; b) where it sits with relation to other processes; c) how critical the process is; d) who owns the process; and e) what is the error resolution for the process. Ultimately, investors will only be satisfied with the operational integrity of a fund if the manager can meet prove that they follow a 3-D view on processes, which means do (as in have the processes in place), document (as in have every detail specified and written down), and demonstrate (as in be able to show any aspect of the process to investors and regulators, for instance during on-site visits).

Infrastructure and Technology

Beyond risk and the 3Ps (people, processes, and procedures), there are also specific infrastructure issues that are important to consider. Of course there is physical infrastructure such as office space and how best to configure it to achieve maximum efficiency. The decisions related to physical infrastructure will largely be driven by cost, business requirements, firm size, geography, and aesthetic considerations. For some hedge fund founders the physical infrastructure decisions might be easy or some might actually find them quite stressful. Either way, it is important to remember that it will likely take some time to find a suitable location and get it fitted out to the required specification.

Part of that renovating and refitting process will be driven by technology needs. Understanding the technology requirements of your hedge fund strategy is critical in ensuring you have the right technology in place, beginning with servers and continuing to workstations and Bloomberg terminals. Regulators and hedge fund investors are focused increasingly on a hedge fund's technological infrastructure and related processes. On the one hand, they want to ensure that a hedge fund has the technological capacity to consistently implement the stated investment strategy. For example, a hedge fund like Renaissance Technologies will have invested significantly more in the technology aspects of their business – both in terms of hardware and software, due to the nature of their investment strategy – than a single-strategy, fundamental-oriented hedge fund which does not trade very frequently. On the other hand, regulators and hedge fund investors also want to confirm that even in situations where there might be a possible disruption to business due to natural disaster or some sort of technology failure, there is a contingency plan in place to allow for business continuity.

The technology discussion above demonstrates the increasing nexus between technology, operational issues, compliance, and regulatory requirements. These are all very important concerns for the hedge fund manager who wants to attract capital from institutional investors and not run foul of regulatory requirements. Properly navigating this aspect of managing a hedge fund requires constant monitoring and will require an investment in time and money.

Fortunately, there are various service providers that a hedge fund can turn to for assistance. In the early stages of a hedge fund's life, a prime broker's business consulting team (or similarly named team) can help with aspects of securing and renovating the physical infrastructure. Additionally, they can also provide assistance on aspects of technology needs as well as introduce specialized information technology specialists who can help with the set-up and maintenance of a hedge fund's information technology infrastructure. A hedge fund that does not want to bring an expensive information technology function in-house might find a third-party information technology service provider more cost-effective and sufficient for its needs.

Given the tremendous amount of financial regulation that has been implemented globally, compliance has become a very important issue. Larger hedge funds will undoubtedly have dedicated compliance staff, however, for start-up hedge funds it is likely prudent to engage compliance consultant. For regulatory and compliance issues, a compliance consultant can assist with regular regulatory issues that might not demand the full service of a law firm and a law firm's associated costs. For some hedge funds, compliance consultants can serve akin to an outsourced compliance officer, while for other firms they serve as a resource for the in-house compliance officer. The compliance consultant industry has grown in lockstep with the rise of financial regulation and can be an important partner for a start-up hedge fund as they can assist from inception (e.g., assisting a start-up hedge fund get licensed in the relevant jurisdictions) to maturity (e.g., assisting with day to day compliance matters that every regulated financial entity has to deal with).

Operations, compliance, and infrastructure demands are becoming increasingly complex and demanding as a result of post-GFC regulations being instituted in multiple jurisdictions. Frankly, ensuring different processes are in order and working to ensure compliance with regulations can be tedious and at times costly. That said, for the hedge fund that is proactive in fulfilling its requirements, operations and similar functions that previously might have been viewed as a cost centre can actually be a differentiating point from its competitors. For the hedge fund seeking capital from institutional investors, robust operations, compliance, and infrastructure is an absolute necessity.

Bibliography

Aikman, J.S. (2010) *When Prime Brokers Fail: The Unheeded Risk to Hedge Funds, Banks, and the Financial Industry.* John Wiley & Sons: Hoboken, NJ.

AIM. (2011) *A Guide to Institutional Investors' Views and Preferences Regarding Hedge Fund Operational Infrastructures.* Alternative Investment Management Association: London.

Berman, M. (ed.) (2007) *Hedge Funds and Prime Brokers.* Risk Books: London.

Strachman, D.A. (2012) *The Fundamentals of Hedge Fund Management: How to Successfully Launch and Operate a Hedge Fund.* John Wiley & Sons: Chichester.

Wilson, R. (2011) *The Hedge Fund Book: A Training Manual for Professionals and Capital Raising Executives.* John Wiley & Sons: Chichester.

PART V
FINAL THOUGHTS

Chapter 10

Investing in Energy Commodity Hedge Funds

Know what you own, and know why you own it.
Peter Lynch

This chapter is useful for individual fund managers as well as asset allocators. Although this chapter is written with asset allocators in mind, it will be helpful for individual fund managers to better understand the need and mind-set of their prospective investors.

As an asset allocator, managing a portfolio of hedge funds and other strategies, you quickly realize that you need to kiss a lot of frogs before finding your prince. Finding quality managers is a painstaking process. We hope that some of the points outlined below will be helpful as you consider adding energy commodity hedge funds to your portfolio.

Initially, we will focus on the broader issues faced by all asset allocators as they seek to build and manage their portfolio. We will then build on that foundation by looking at the specific issues investors should be aware of when building a portfolio in this space.

Asset Allocation: Portfolio Building Basics

You may be an endowment, family office, fund of funds, or other large pool of capital seeking to build a portfolio of alternative investment managers that ideally provide superior investment performance while minimizing volatility found in the normal market. As part of your portfolio construction process, you may be considering different geographies, investment strategies, underlying asset classes, investment horizons, liquidity needs, and a myriad of other factors. Though this evaluation process is a necessity for any serious asset allocator, the outcome of such an exercise will likely be different for each institution. A family office may have greater liquidity needs in the short run, while an endowment may not need their allocated capital for seven years. An insurance company in Asia, with a stable revenue base in Asia, may feel a desire to allocate away from Asia and focus on Europe and North America. Each institution that is contemplating allocating to an alternative investment manager will have *sui generis* needs, so it is absolutely necessary to be thoughtful about the parameters of such an allocation programme for it to be successful.

Once the desired portfolio has been mapped out, the hard work really begins. Building and managing a successful portfolio of alternative investment managers requires three contemporaneously ongoing activities:

1. manager selection
2. due diligence
3. monitoring.

Manager selection is the prince or princess kissing the frog portion of the process. Like most investment processes, screening opportunities is a numbers game. An organization looking to allocate capital will end up meeting countless managers before finding a select few to build a portfolio with. Meeting with managers will be an ongoing process and many experienced asset allocators have a database of hundreds, if not thousands, of firms across different investment strategies they have met over the years. Of this number, only a small handful of the investment managers an asset allocator has met will actually receive capital. This fact conveys that for both asset allocators and investment managers, manager selection is a time-consuming but frequently unavoidable process.

Manager selection will usually start with a meeting or conference call that reviews the basics of the investment manager's strategy, investment performance, the team, and other basic questions. These meetings can be initiated via a capital introduction person at a prime broker, through a third-party marketer, through personal connections or referrals, or a whole host of other methods. The asset allocator will often be asked to be included on any distribution lists the investment manager operates (e.g., monthly newsletter). If an asset allocator is potentially interested, they will ask for more raw data to conduct their own analysis. If the interest continues, this will be followed up by further meetings in person. If interest persists, sophisticated allocators will conduct due diligence. On the quick side, from first meeting to allocation, it could only take a few weeks, however, in the post-2008 GFC, post-Madoff world that we operate in today, the decision to allocate usually takes a few months and could potentially take a few years.

For example, a pension may like a particular fund manager but be a bit concerned because the fund's track record is only two years and the size of the fund is still under USD 100 million. These points notwithstanding, the pension fund would still potentially like to make an allocation at some point, so it continues to track the fund manager by having quarterly calls, receiving the monthly newsletter, and staying abreast of the manager's growth. Then, when the fund manager's track record hits four years and the fund's size is close to USD 200 million, the pension may decide to allocate.

The decision to allocate is almost always preceded by a period of due diligence, which may include at least one, if not multiple, visit(s) by the investor to the fund manager's office for a few hours. This due diligence might be incredibly thorough and protracted or be brief, with capital allocated shortly after the decision to allocate has been made. Investors will have slightly different approaches depending on their risk profiles, internal resources, their own investor base, and their performance history. Larger institutions, such as well-established university endowments, will have much of the due diligence capability existing in-house, while institutions with fewer resources might rely on investment consultants to perform screening and due diligence.

Generally speaking, if an asset allocator has committed to performing due diligence, then the fund and its manager have passed the initial 'sniff' test. The performance of the fund, the investment strategy, and the background of the fund manager and his team have satisfied the initial litmus test. Due diligence is conducted to make sure that what has been presented is in fact the truth, to uncover any potential risk factors that have not fully been explored, and to ensure the investor has a comprehensive understanding and comfort with any potential investment they might make. As a fund manager, if your fund has reached this stage then you are on the right path.

To help facilitate this process, most fund managers typically prepare what is commonly called a due diligence questionnaire, as discussed above (please review Appendix C to get a general sense of what a DDQ entails). Each fund may approach preparation of a DDQ differently. Some funds will have one Bible-like DDQ where all information is compiled into one extensive document. This can be convenient since all pertinent information is found in one document and only that document needs to be updated. Alternatively, some firms prefer to separate their DDQs topically. For example, a performance and investment-related DDQ, an operationally oriented DDQ, etc. After carefully considering what works best for a fund and its strategy, a fund manager should select the DDQ style that works best for their particular fund and its investment style.

Regardless of what form a DDQ takes, it should be thorough and updated on a regular basis. At the very least, compiling a DDQ forces the fund manager to think of how best to present factual information to potential investors. This is a useful exercise that will help in both better managing the investment firm as a business enterprise as well as assisting in marketing efforts. Most experienced investors in hedge funds will ask for a DDQ, so it is better to start earlier rather than later on organizing a comprehensive DDQ.

From the perspective of an entity investing in energy commodity hedge funds, a DDQ is a key resource in conducting thorough due diligence. In particular, the background of the fund manager and his team, proper understanding of investment performance, and operational competency are extremely critical when evaluating many energy commodity hedge fund strategies. Given the use of derivatives and sometimes more complex strategies used by energy commodity hedge funds, a DDQ provides insight into how the investment manager thinks about risk and whether they grasp what some of the key risk issues might be.

Assuming a fund manager successfully navigates the due diligence process and is allocated capital by an investor, the next stage is monitoring. As a fund manager might monitor a portfolio of stocks, an investor of hedge funds also manages a portfolio of hedge funds. Some asset allocators may require extensive transparency so they can manage their risk on a real-time basis, while other allocators may take a more laissez-faire approach and only expect updates on a monthly or quarterly basis with minimal visibility of the portfolio. Much of this will be driven by the liquidity requirements, risk profile, and investment timeline of the asset allocator.

From a client service perspective, a fund manager should be ready to accommodate all reasonable requests from an investor once capital has been accepted. As a general principle, good communication and transparency lead to long-term partnerships that are mutually beneficial. Obviously, good investment performance during that time does not hurt either. At the very least, a fund manager should be prepared to write monthly or quarterly newsletters to be circulated to clients and prospective clients. Good examples of these types of investor communication are letters written by Warren Buffet to Berkshire Hathaway investors or by Howard Marks to Oaktree Capital investors. Besides letters, fund managers should be prepared to have regular conference calls as well as possible face-to-face meetings with investors both during good times as well as difficult times.

The reality is that at some point, redemption of capital is a fact of hedge fund life. The process by which redemptions occur, when they occur, and whether a particular investor reallocates capital to a fund manager is not solely driven by fund performance. For investors that have an institutionalized investment process, redemptions may very likely be dictated by results obtained from initial due diligence before the investment. During due diligence prior to the investment, certain redemption triggers may have been identified and when one those triggers are tripped redemptions may follow. Often these redemption triggers may have nothing to do with performance but can be due to factors such as staff turnover, changes in investment strategy, large redemptions that decrease AUM of the fund to a certain level, etc.

Though performance is a major factor, it is important to remember that this is still a people business where relationships are built on trust. Fund managers who have built deep relationships built on trust, placing clients' interests first, and proactive communication will find their lives are easier during difficult times and when raising capital.

Asset Allocation: Understanding Different Strategies

In this section, we begin by reviewing the typical energy commodity hedge fund strategies. We then analyse investment considerations particular to energy commodities, such as:

- Whether to invest in energy commodities at all.
- Market maturity (developed regulatory regime?).
- Energy commodity market capacity constraints.
- Skill bottleneck: skill specificity requirements and the time-consuming growth of energy trading talent.
- Volatility.
- Correlation.

Typical Energy Commodity Hedge Fund Strategies

Let us quickly review the two fundamental types of trading: fundamental and technical. Fundamental analysis-based trading is based on quantitative and qualitative analysis of the underlying physical analysis of the market. Technical trading is based on quantitative analysis, in essence tracking past market behaviour through computer-based statistical modelling programs.

When categorizing typical energy commodity hedge fund strategies we can categorize them into two broad categories: directional trading and relative value trading. As its name suggests, directional trading takes a view on what direction the price of a given commodity will follow, and takes a position accordingly, being long products expected to rise or short those expected to fall. Relative value trading aims to exploit pricing inefficiencies between different products and different time horizons. In essence, relative value trades identify products whose prices are expected to converge over a certain period of time, being long the underpriced product and short the overpriced one.

Generally, certain energy commodity markets have been around for considerably less time than equity or bond markets. This means there is an element of regulatory uncertainty around certain types of product. This is particularly true of emission allowances. Having said that, the upside of their youth is that energy commodity markets are less regulated than traditional investment markets such as equities. This enables traders to be more imaginative and innovative in their strategies.

Two 'bottlenecks' make it particularly challenging for investors to locate potential investments: the scarcity of excellent energy traders and the limited capital which may be prudently deployed by trading any particular energy commodity strategy. Many traders seem to be of equal skill, but there are traders who clearly distinguish themselves from others.

Energy Commodity Market Capacity Constraints

Compared with many other hedge fund markets, there are not many excellent start-up or early-stage funds to invest in within the energy commodity space. Furthermore, those that exist are often unable to absorb additional capital. This inability to accept additional capital may be driven by a fund's own success, being able to leverage existing investors, or increasing the proportion of the fund manager's own money. In some extremes, very successful energy commodity funds return considerable portions of their AUM to their investors year after year in impressive double-digit returns. At the heart of these capital capacity constraints lie two limitations. The first is a limit particular to each fund. Every fund manager will have a maximum amount of capital he feels comfortable investing, as constrained by his own intellectual capital bandwidth and that of his team. Second, there is a limit to how much capital can be safely deployed within a given market, as defined by the market size, competitive dynamics, competitor fragmentation, liquidity, and regulation. There will come a point in every market where a position is large enough to move the market, or where positions of a certain size become 'too visible' to competitors. The capacity constraints are exacerbated in energy commodity markets given their size and the small number of players that regularly trade them. Accordingly, a key consideration for any investor must be the capacity to expand.

The lack of investment capacity places a premium on an established network of contacts in the energy commodity business. An investor research analyst will need to personally cultivate many relationships within the energy commodity trading community in order to secure capacity in high-quality funds. Furthermore, these relationships will be necessary to conduct due diligence, understand the relevant markets and their evolution, and ensure that any aspiring fund manager will contact them very early in the planning process for a new fund.

Skill Shortage

The dramatic growth of energy commodity markets has outstripped the availability of talent capable of wisely trading these markets. Utilities and energy producers continue to employ the vast majority of the knowledgeable energy commodity talent. Many of these institutions and their employees, however, do not have the financial and trading skills to appropriately deploy risk capital. When it comes to non-knowledgeable talent, the extreme complexity of the markets does not facilitate the quick redeployment of a non-energy trader such as a currency or bond trader. The migration of utility and producer employees to banks, hedge funds, and other financial investors continues at a growing pace. Nevertheless, it is not growing at a fast enough pace to meet demand. Furthermore, utilities and producers are increasing the financial training offered to their staff, and developing in-house capabilities to slow down the migration.

The authors briefly discussed earlier the most important trading strategies and their relevant implications for successful hedge fund managers. We maintain that a portfolio of energy commodity hedge funds should take into consideration different product mixes (e.g., gas, power, oil), different fund manager maturities, different trading styles and strategies (e.g., financial vs. physical, long only, relative value), as well as different geographic exposures (e.g. Europe and North America). While it is well known that start-up and early-stage funds have a high attrition rate, it must not be forgotten that larger funds with established track records (e.g., Amaranth as discussed in the Introduction) often cost investors much more money when their strategies fail or disappoint. Talented early-stage managers can often deliver higher returns – if they are successful. On the contrary, larger, more mature funds can often afford greater investment in research and risk management systems.

Much has been written on portfolio measurement and risk management for investors. The structure of the markets in which these funds invest is often rapidly changing in response to ongoing deregulation or liberalization, as well as the introduction of new mechanisms such as the trading of emission allowances. A fund manager who has performed well in the past may not adapt well or quickly to changing markets. This can be costly to investors. As such, ongoing 'market due diligence' and research is required.

Finally, as investors consider allocating to an energy commodity hedge fund they must be acutely aware of both volatility and correlation. The ideal hedge fund strategy is capital appreciative and capital protective. Too much volatility in a fund's performance can erode its capital base. Additionally, a fund with performance that is largely index correlative or market tracking not only lacks true alpha opportunities but is also costing investors since it is an expensive form of beta. If an investor is paying hedge fund fees to invest in a hedge fund product, they should seek a product that is more than an expensive exchange-traded fund (ETF) or market-correlation product. Thus, a prospective fund needs to be valuated in conjunction with an understanding of the fund's risk-adjusted performance, volatility, and correlation.

There are technical measures that should be considered when constructing a portfolio that includes an energy commodity hedge fund. An energy commodity hedge fund may be part of a larger portfolio of energy-oriented investments or may be part of a hedge fund portfolio that includes a wide range of strategies and geographies – where energy commodities are just part of the portfolio. Depending on the niche it fills, different technical measures may be used to measure and balance the portfolio. Being thoughtful about the role an energy commodity hedge fund satisfies in a portfolio is important to ensure the right manager is selected, the right perspective is taken when constructing the portfolio, and the right measures are used to monitor the portfolio's performance.

Checklist for Investing in Energy Commodity Hedge Funds

Though this checklist is not exhaustive, it serves as a starting point for an investor considering an investment in an energy commodity hedge fund.

- ☐ Clear Understanding of the Investment Strategy
    - ☐ Does the strategy make sense?
    - ☐ Does it correspond with what is visible in the world today?
- ☐ Portfolio Construction and Concentration
    - ☐ How is the portfolio constructed?
    - ☐ How concentrated is the portfolio?
- ☐ Strategy Liquidity
    - ☐ How liquid is the portfolio?
    - ☐ Does it meet our required liquidity needs?
    - ☐ Has liquidity been considered in worst-case situations (i.e., 2008)?

☐ Is the underlying market liquid enough to efficiently facilitate the style of trading the hedge fund manager is planning?

☐ Use of Derivatives
  ☐ Does the strategy rely heavily on derivatives?
  ☐ If so, is investment risk and operational risk properly accounted for?
  ☐ How capable is the fund manager with using derivatives?
  ☐ Is there a better way to express the strategy than with derivatives?

☐ Strategy Capacity Issues
  ☐ What aspects of the market may prevent this strategy from being successful?
  ☐ At what size (in terms of assets under management) will it become difficult to execute the investment strategy?

☐ Regulatory Environment
  ☐ What is the regulatory environment for the particular energy asset?
  ☐ Is it changing?
  ☐ Is it political?

☐ Experience of Fund Manager and Team
  ☐ Do the fund manager and his team have experience successfully running this strategy?
  ☐ How do they source/identify investment opportunities?
  ☐ Are they smart?
  ☐ Are they honest?
  ☐ Are they humble?
  ☐ Will they be good partners?
  ☐ What do people say about them? Do they have good references?

☐ Fees
  ☐ Are the fees fair/market standard?
  ☐ Given performance, volatility, and correlation are the fees worth it for this product?

☐ Side Letters
  ☐ If possible to find out, have other investors signed side letters giving them a different fee structure or other benefits?
  ☐ If so, will I be disadvantaged investing in this fund vis-à-vis the other investors?

Bibliography

Bauer, C., Heidorn T., and Kaiser, D. (2012) A Primer on Commodity Hedge Funds. *Journal of Derivatives & Hedge Funds* 18, 223-235.

Bernstein, W. (2000) *The Intelligent Asset Allocator: How to Build Your Portfolio to Maximize Returns and Minimize Risk*. McGraw-Hill: New York.

Grinold, R. (1999) *Active Portfolio Management: A Quantitative Approach for Producing Superior Returns and Selecting Superior Returns and Controlling Risk*. McGraw-Hill: New York.

Maginn, J.L., *et al.* (2007) *Managing Investment Portfolios: A Dynamic Process*. John Wiley & Sons: Hoboken, NJ.

Shain, R. (2008) *Hedge Fund Due Diligence*. John Wiley & Sons: Hoboken, NJ.

Scharfman, J.A. (2008) *Hedge Fund Operational Due Diligence*. John Wiley & Sons: Chichester.

Snopek, L. (2012) *The Complete Guide to Portfolio Construction and Management*. John Wiley & Sons: Chichester.

Swensen, D. (2009) *Pioneering Portfolio Management: An Unconventional Approach to Institutional Investment*. Free Press: New York.

Chapter 11

Quo Vadis

The best thing about the future is that it comes only one day at a time.
Abraham Lincoln

1. *Will there be further political and regulatory intervention in a way that is harmful to energy hedge funds and their growth?*

When considering regulatory intervention and energy hedge funds, there are three broad themes: (1) regulation of energy hedge funds; (2) regulation of commodities trading (physical and financial); and (3) regulation of other players in the market.

From what we can tell, there do not appear to be any new political or regulatory initiatives that are specifically targeting energy hedge funds. Following the GFC, position limits that were designed to limit speculation in commodity markets were introduced as part of the Dodd–Frank Wall Street Reform and Consumer Protection Act. Dodd–Frank was signed into law on 21 July 2010. Following the enactment of Dodd–Frank, the Commodity Futures Trading Commission (CFTC) introduced rules on position limits for futures and swaps. In response to a civil action brought by the International Swaps and Derivatives Association, the US District Court for the District of Columbia issued an order on 28 September 2012 that essentially nullified the CFTC's position limit rules and required the CFTC to reconsider new position limit policies, which have not been finalized as of yet.

That said, regulations that impact hedge funds broadly will obviously affect energy hedge funds as well. For example, over the last few years we have seen different regulations emerge such as the Alternative Investment Fund Managers Directive (AIFMD) in Europe, which is not focused on energy hedge funds, but will by default encompass energy hedge funds that have a European nexus. These types of broader regulation that capture hedge funds in their scope will influence energy hedge funds.

Beyond increased regulation of hedge funds, regulation of the actual commodities markets has not been significant in the last few years. Besides a burgeoning of the renewable energy and emissions market, the structure of the market for traditional commodities remains fairly stable. The CFTC has taken on a more high-profile role following the GFC but regulation, particularly of the physical markets, has not changed meaningfully. On the non-physical side of commodities trading, different regulations focused on reducing OTC derivative risk may impact energy hedge funds as OTC market participants across asset classes (equities, credit, commodities, FX, etc.) are increasingly being pushed to standardize OTC derivatives documentation in order to facilitate electronic confirmation and central clearing.

New regulations over the last few years have focused on investment banks and similar financial institutions that were robust market participants in various commodities markets. These new regulations are shaping the participation of these institutions in commodities markets. This will be discussed further in the next question.

2. *What will be the impact of hedge funds closing down and the retrenchment of the banks from commodities?*

In recent years, there has been a consistent theme of investment banks retreating from their respective commodities businesses as they look to focus on core business areas that may be less balance sheet intensive in the wake of Basel III and other similar regulatory policies. One major change to futures business is the fact that – as of mid-2014 – the margin posted by clients and kept on balance sheet by the banks will be considered 'equity' of the firm, greatly reducing the return on equity (RoE) measures that analysts use when evaluating banks. Therefore, most banks will charge interest on these margin amounts, at which point they can be reclassified and taken off the balance sheet. Most banks will make up for this new charge by charging less in other areas and attempt to keep most clients equal in terms of overall cost or fee load. Although in general we are supporters of increased regulation, we believe new policies must achieve specific goals. In this case, this one consequence of Basel III seems to be a value-destroying endeavour in terms of human time and cost without significantly improving the stability of the global financial markets.

This significant change in the make up of commodity markets in terms of the nature of their major participants should provide greater opportunities for new commodity hedge funds to enter the marketplace. Additionally, existing commodity hedge funds should also be in a position to benefit from this structural shift. There will be opportunities to fill the void that has been created by the exit of banks from the commodities market. A significant amount of risk that banks used to warehouse is now up for grabs by market participants that have the appetite and sophistication to do so. Additionally, we should see a proliferation of different types of commodities strategy from commodity hedge funds that are focused on trading less liquid strategies – almost private equity style – which may include a financing component and/or a warehousing component in the trade.

3. *How will the relationship between energy hedge funds and energy private equity funds evolve? Does the nomenclature define a distinction without a difference?*

Fundamentally, we feel that investment firms which can blend aspects from the private equity world's focus on investing in assets with the ability of hedge funds to trade around positions should excel in the commodities marketplace going forward.

Owing to the primacy of liquidity immediately following the GFC, this type of hybrid strategy was not attractive. As the memory of the crisis fades and the emphasis on liquidity wanes, investment firms that can convey the benefits of a hybrid strategy will be in a much better position to raise capital for their commodity strategies.

Although commodities' expertise can be found among both private equity and hedge fund investors, the investment toolkit required to successfully deploy a hybrid strategy requires specialized knowledge that spans both worlds. This will normally require different investment professionals and teams with such specialist knowledge. Additionally, beyond just specific investment know-how, a hybrid strategy also requires a management team that understands the requirements of successfully implementing both types of investment strategy and can act as a bridge between the two worlds. The inherent trade-offs in terms of return drivers between assets and risk positions must be managed in order to maximize returns. This holistic view is the key to success.

Structurally, and from a business strategy perspective, we do not expect a renaissance of hybrid vehicles, but the emergence of vertically integrated offerings by asset management firms. In such a proposition, firms will offer a beta product, a hedge fund product (with more of a relative value focus), a commodity financing product, and a private equity product more related to warehousing and/or infrastructure. They will however be distinct value propositions and products, attracting investment from varied investor types and different 'asset allocation buckets'.

4. *Will 'energy-environmental' hedge funds be enablers of positive climate change or impediments to the success of Kyoto and other market-based regimes?*

We strongly feel that market forces and, by extension, market participants play a critical role in addressing the environmental issues that society faces today, including climate change. Market tools are one prong of a multi-pronged solution to address such issues. For example, the EU ETS has created a robust 'cap and trade' system that despite various growing pains and criticisms continues to evolve as a key part of how the EU is addressing greenhouse gas emissions. Admittedly, these structures are far from perfect but we feel that over time, market participants that are active within these types of regulatory framework will positively contribute to addressing the negative effects of climate change. In order for this to occur, however, market participation must be better regulated, better reported, and better monitored in order to avoid abuse of the system.

5. *Other than prime brokers, hedge fund managers, and investors, who are the net winners and losers from the presence of energy hedge funds in the market?*

If market mechanisms are working correctly, over the long run it is consumers that should benefit from an energy market that has an increased number of market participants. Consumers should be beneficiaries of lower prices and as more participants enter the market, the market should become deeper and more liquid with more efficient price discovery. Consumers should also benefit from lower volatility. Subtly, it is not market participants that have a dampening effect on volatility, but the number of market participants that have different rationales and trading styles. For instance, in 2006-2008, there was arguably a record number of market participants in crude oil, but they were all focusing on long-holdings in the front month, which drove volatility higher. A variety of market participants is also key and regulators should encourage all sorts of players to participate in the market, from consumers and producers, to speculators and liquidity providers.

6. *What is the future for energy hedge funds?*

Generally, energy hedge funds have followed the prevailing trends of the broader hedge fund industry as a whole.

Currently, institutionalization is the key theme from an operational business perspective (including regulation and compliance); alongside tight and disciplined risk management, which is top of mind in energy and commodity strategies given their typically higher volatility profiles. In practice, this means that players with mature infrastructure and a focus on drawdown management are being rewarded. Following the GFC, there was a flight to size and brand, as these hedge fund managers most easily ticked the right boxes for institutional investors. These hedge fund managers, however, are often constrained by their size. Their size can sometimes make it difficult to efficiently exercise the desired strategy. It is widely accepted in the industry that size is frequently an enemy of performance, with larger funds losing the nimbleness they require to successfully navigate markets and generate profit.

We feel that this trend, however, is starting to shift as people realize there is a clear inverse correlation between size and assets. Hedge fund behemoths have failed to deliver returns and have increasingly become asset-gathering machines focused on generating revenue from collecting management fees.

On the back of quantitative easing (QE) policies, US equity markets have been exceptionally buoyant the last few years. The market dynamics of the last few years have made it difficult for many macro strategies, including commodities and energy strategies, to deliver consistent performance, especially on a relative basis when compared with equity markets and even bonds.

As QE comes to a gradual end, commodities should play a key role in portfolio construction for a number of reasons:

1. The historically low correlation between commodities and equities and fixed income.

2. The role of commodities as an inflation hedge given the prospect of increasing inflation (we should point out that there is strong differing opinions on data supporting causality, especially if we believe that the next few years will be an era of asset price inflation due to monetary policy as opposed to inflation due to – artificial – scarcity such as the driver of oil price shocks in the 1970s).

3. The structural demand for commodities in China and emerging markets.

4. In the near to medium term there will likely be a transition in the business cycle towards the latter part of the expansionary cycle, which has historically been the portion of the business cycle where commodities have generally performed well, particularly in the wake of a recession (we caveat this by asking whether this is a historically "normal" business cycle given the technological revolution we are in the early stages, which may mean less capital is needed to provide a historic level of return (e.g., US corporate returns for the past four years), so capital formation will be running below historic averages and this may lead to lower commodity demand than in the past).

The first green sprouts confirming such an upbeat prediction have materialized in 2014:

- In the first six months of 2014, commodities were one of the strongest performing asset classes and a great diversifier against the lesser performance of equities; some of the commodity strategies such as passive beta benchmarks (GSCI or DJUBS CI) are up on the year for the first time in a while.
- There has been a fall in correlation among commodity markets themselves and versus other asset classes as differentiation across individual commodities is again largely driven by individual commodity supply and demand dynamics rather than macro risk on/risk off dynamics that tend to drive correlations to one.
- Some commodities such as oil have returned to a state of structural backwardation, suggesting positive carry may help push returns up for investors with exposure to commodity futures markets.
- The aforementioned decrease in market participation by regulated entities such as banks and other asset managers may lead to less competition that in turn may make it easier to identify and execute trading opportunities.
- Increased speculation that inflation pressure may take hold in developed markets may make investors enthusiastic about putting on commodity-related inflation hedging risk.
- The emergence of macro themes around increases in geopolitical risk or emerging market performance issues may help the return of price trends and volatility across commodity markets.

Hedge funds will continue to be a key player in the investment universe, attempting to deliver alpha and boost investor portfolios. Energy hedge funds and commodities as a whole should return to being considered a great diversifier for a traditional 60/40 balanced portfolio. The increase in correlation that commodity assets witnessed versus equities and bonds during the GFC has now subsided.

Investors would be wise to return to a significant allocation to commodities to improve the risk/return profile of their portfolios. Energy hedge funds will have to continue to institutionalize and professionalize their process. Those who do so will differentiate themselves from the crowd and grow to become market leaders. The increase in barriers to entry to the hedge fund market and the rising minimum efficiency scale driven by increasing cost and complexity will sadly reward large firms and unintentionally increase the systemic risk by consolidating the industry into a smaller number of larger players.

Having said that, through strong innovation smaller players can disrupt the market and continue to thrive as lean organizations that are more nimble and can therefore outperform their bigger competitors. Although the years since the GFC have not been the best for the industry, the trough has likely reached its nadir in 2014 and it is an opportune time to invest in the energy commodity asset class.

Bibliography

For papers on the impact of position limits for futures and swaps, please refer to the following link hosted on the CFTC website: www.cftc.gov/LawRegulation/DoddFrankAct/Rulemakings/DF_26_PosLimits/positionlimitstudies.

Baxter, M., Di Marzo, A., Joshi, A. and de Gooyer, C. (2012) *New Rules of the Road for Banks: Overcoming the Regulatory Challenges to Growth.* Bain & Company: Boston, MA.

Goldman Sachs (2014) Commodities Research. The Strategic Case for Commodities Holding Strong.

International Swaps and Derivatives Association v. United States Commodity Futures Trading Commission, 887 F. Supp. 2d 259 (D.D.C. 2012).

McKinsey & Co (2012) Global Corporate and Investment Banking: An Agenda for Change.

Morgan Stanley & Oliver Wyman (2014) Wholesale & Investment Banking Outlook, Blue Paper, 20 March.

Quigley, S. (2009) Hybrid appetite rapacious: hybrid private equity. Available at: www.risk.net/hedge-funds-review/feature/2247744/hybrid-appetite-rapacious-hybrid-private-equity.

Shadab, H.B. (2009) Coming together after the crisis: Global convergence of private equity and hedge funds. *Northwestern Journal of International Law & Business* 29(3), 603–616.

Appendix A

Sample Business Plan Outline

As described in Chapter 5, a business plan will have multiple uses during the early stages of a hedge fund's life. Initially, a business plan will likely serve as a planning document for the hedge fund founder. Later, during licensing or registering procedures, regulators will often ask for a business plan. The business plan that might be required by a regulator will likely focus on different aspects of the business and be more focused on demonstrating that regulatory requirements have been accounted for. Further, much of the information in a hedge fund's business plan will eventually find its way into a fund's PPM (see Appendix B) and due diligence questionnaire (see Appendix C). The outline below provides a menu of options for an aspiring hedge fund manager to consider, including when creating a business plan.

1. Cover Page
2. Table of Contents
3. Introduction: Nature and Scope of Business
   (a) Industry Overview
   (b) Investment Philosophy and Strategy
   (c) Relevant Experience and Historical Performance
4. Risk Management
   (a) Market Risk
      (i) Identify Market Risk Factors
      (ii) Risk Systems, Use of Hedging, and Other Risk Management Tools
   (b) Operational Risk
      (i) Identify Operational Risk Factors
5. Team
   (a) Biographical Information of Key Team Members
   (b) Organizational Chart
6. Clients and Business Development
   (a) Current and Prospective Clients
      (i) How Will Clients Be Serviced?

     (ii) How Much Transparency Will Clients Have?
     (iii) How Frequently and With What Method(s) Will Clients Be Contacted?
         1. Newsletter Monthly, quarterly, or other interval of time?
         2. Valuation Updates? If so, how frequently?
  (b) Distribution Channels
  (c) Fee Structure
  (d) Fundraising Targets and Timeline
  (e) Contingencies if Fundraising Targets Not Met
7. Ownership Details of the Investment Firm
  (a) Ownership Chart
  (b) Background Information on Non-Employee Shareholders
8. Management and Corporate Governance
  (a) Key Company Details (Contact Information, Incorporation Date, Jurisdiction of Incorporation, etc.)
  (b) Biographical Information on Corporate Directors
  (c) Cash Flow Planning and Financial Resources
     (i) Inventory of Company Financial Resources
     (ii) Budget
         1. Monthly Operating Budget
         2. Yearly Operating Budget
     (iii) Revenue Needed to Reach Break-Even Point
     (iv) Sources of Revenue
  (d) Key Man Provisions
  (e) Business Continuity Planning
9. Service Providers
  (a) Administrator
  (b) Audit
  (c) Custodian
  (d) Execution Broker(s)
  (e) Legal
  (f) Prime Broker(s)
10. Compliance, Legal, and Regulatory
  (a) Required Licences?
     (i) Process and Timeline to Receive Licences
     (ii) Ongoing Requirements to Maintain Licence
  (b) Compliance Procedures
     (i) Anti-Money Laundering
     (ii) Compliance Manual and Policies
     (iii) Conflicts of Interest
     (iv) Know Your Client
     (v) Segregation of Duties
     (vi) System for Record Keeping

Appendix B

Outline of a Confidential Explanatory Memorandum: Sample Offshore Feeder Ltd

[Explanatory Information and Related Disclaimers]

Table of Contents

SAMPLE OFFSHORE FEEDER LTD

SUMMARY OF TERMS

The following is a summary of this document and other documents relating to the Fund. This document and related agreements should be reviewed carefully for more information with respect to the Fund.

The Fund

Investment Objective

The Investment Manager

Risk Factors

Shares

The Offering

Management Fee

Incentive Allocation

Expenses

Redemptions

Reports

Board of Directors

Tax Status

DIRECTORY

Registered Office:

Investment Manager:

Administrator:

Sub-Administrator

Auditors:

Clearing Brokers:

Corporate Secretary:

United States Counsel:

Cayman Islands Counsel:

1. **The Fund – Organizational Structure**
   Description of Sample Offshore Feeder and Organizational Structure

2. **Investment Objective**
   Investment Objective
   Investment Strategy
   Investment Implementation
   General

3. **Risk Factors**
   Absence of Regulatory Oversight
   Absence of Secondary Market
   Accounting for Uncertainty in Income Taxes
   Amortization of Organizational Costs
   Availability of Investment Strategies
   Business Risk
   Calculation of Net Asset Value

Clearing Brokers
Clearing Brokers and Broker Insolvency
Clearing Brokers to the Master Fund
Custody Risk
Clearing House Protections
Collateral
Commodities Risk
Commodity and Futures Contracts
Concentration of Investments
Contingent Liability Transactions
Counterparty and Settlement Risk
Currency Exposure
Derivatives
Dividends and Distributions
Early Costs and Losses
Economic Conditions
Foreign Taxation
Forward Foreign Exchange Contracts
Futures
Gapping
Highly Volatile Markets
Incentive Allocation
Inventory Levels of Underlying Metal Commodities
Access to Investment Manager Investment Professionals and Fund
Information
Insolvency
Investment Objective
Leverage
Limited Operating History
Liquidity and Market Characteristics
Liquidity on Odd Dates
Management Risk
Market Crisis and Governmental Intervention
Market Liquidity and Leverage
Market Risk
Nature of Investments
Net Asset Value Considerations
No Separate Counsel; No Responsibility or Independent Verification
Operating Deficits
Operational Risks and Business Disruptions
Options
Options Trading

Portfolio Concentration
Price Fluctuations
Regulatory Risks of Private Funds
Reliance on Management
Risk Control Framework
Short Selling
Side Letters
Speculative Position Limits
Substantial Redemptions
Swap Agreements
Systems Risks
Trading in Commodities and Other Investments May Be Illiquid
Transaction Costs
Volatility

4. **Management**
Investment Manager

5. **Conflicts of Interest**

6. **Investment Management Agreement**
Management Fee
Incentive Allocation
Other Terms of the Investment Management Agreement

7. **Description of Common Shares**
General
Special Designation as Non-Voting Common Shares
Exclusive Voting Rights in Respect of Reserved Matters

8. **Offering of Common Shares**
Offering Price

9. **Redemptions**
Key Person Event
Compulsory Redemption
Suspension of Redemption Rights

10. **Net Asset Value**
Certain Taxation and ERISA Matters
Certain Cayman Islands Tax Considerations
Taxation of the Fund
United States Taxes
US Shareholders – Special Considerations
 PFIC Status

Appendix C

Sample Due Diligence Questionnaire Outline

Please find a sample DDQ outline below. DDQs are not sacrosanct and the below outline is not infallible either. It is provided solely as a reference and can be useful to the new hedge fund manager thinking about preparing a DDQ or a prospective hedge fund investor reviewing a DDQ.

Generally, most DDQs cover similar types of information though each will have its own flavour depending on the investment strategy, characteristics of the fund, and other similar factors. The DDQs created by the AIMA are generally considered industry standard and may be a good starting point as one thinks about creating a DDQ.[13] Remember, however, DDQs are flexible and should be presented in a way that conveys the required information most effectively. For example, a DDQ can be one document or can be separated into individual documents based on topic.

Each fund should have its own DDQ and most of the information found in a DDQ should have significant overlap with information found in a fund's PPM. Additionally, potential hedge fund investors may have their own in-house DDQs that they prefer hedge funds to complete in order to focus on issues they have identified as important.

DDQ Outline

1. Key Information on the Investment Management Group (IMG)
   (a) Investment Manager/Investment Adviser
      (i) Depending on the structure of a hedge fund, an IMG will include the Investment Manager (IM) and may also include an Investment Advisor (IA). For ease, and to avoid confusion, we will use IMG to represent both the IM and the IA, as the case may be.

---

13   Please see AIMA website (www.aima.org) for additional information.

(b) Contact Details
    (i) Contact details should include the following information for the IMG: firm name, address, phone number, fax number, email address, and website address (if applicable).
    (ii) Contact details for key individuals such as the portfolio manager or head of marketing should also be included.

(c) Background of IMG
    (i) At the minimum, background information should include key legal information. For example, what is the legal structure of the IMG? Is it a corporation or a partnership? Where are the respective IMG entities incorporated?
    (ii) Additionally, regulatory information pertaining to the IMG should be included as well. Which regulators have oversight over the IMG? When did the IMG receive its regulatory status/ licences? Is the IMG subject to any regulatory restrictions or exemptions? Has the IMG ever been subject to any regulatory investigations?
    (iii) What types of business activity is the IMG involved in?
    (iv) Chart that denotes the organizational structure of the IMG. This can usually be done by providing an organizational chart that shows division of responsibilities among teams and employees, identifies key personnel (including corporate directors), and where employees and offices are located if the IMG has more than one office. Important to note that if an IMG is operating in multiple jurisdictions then it likely has local entities in various jurisdictions that will be incorporated separately and regulated by local regulators. All of this information should be reflected properly.
    (v) Further information regarding employees should also be provided, such as total number of employees and biographical information on key employees including the portfolio manager and other key investment, risk, and operations professionals. For biographical information, prospective investors generally want to see educational background, type of professional experience, and length of professional experience.
    (vi) A DDQ should also include an ownership chart that identifies the shareholders of the IMG. Employee ownership should be highlighted and an explanation should be provided if the ownership structure is not self-explanatory. Such an explanation should include a brief background of shareholders and their relationship to the IMG if not provided elsewhere in the DDQ.

(vii) Many investors that allocate capital to hedge funds will normally request audited financial statements from at least the last three years.

(d) IMG Client Information

(i) What is the value of the assets that the IMG manages or advises?

(ii) What is the breakdown of investor by category (e.g., endowments, fund of funds, family office, etc.)?

(iii) What is the geographic breakdown of investors?

(iv) What percentage of assets that are managed or advised by the IMG is attributable to the IMG's largest single investor?

2. Investment Management: Research and Trading

(a) Research and Investment Process

(i) Provide a description of how ideas are sourced and then executed. This should include common sources of idea generation and then the process by which an idea becomes an investable idea.

(ii) Some questions worth considering: How are recommendations tracked? Are research notes required to initiate a trade? Does the idea have to be presented to a committee? Who has the decision-making authority to make buy or sell decisions? If an investment is made, how is the position monitored?

(b) Trading

(i) Who are the authorized traders at the IMG? Is there a designated execution trader or team?

(ii) If there is a designated execution trader or team it is recommended to provide relevant points about their background.

(iii) How are trades made and recorded?

(iv) How are trades allocated across multiple portfolios that may have similar strategies? This answer requires a description of the IMG's trade allocation policy.

3. Risk Management, Operations, and Infrastructure

(a) Risk Management

(i) Who is responsible for risk management? What is their background if not detailed elsewhere?

(ii) What are the key risks related to the IMG's investment strategy?

(iii) Describe the IMG's risk management framework including loss limits, position size, portfolio monitoring, liquidity, etc.

(iv) Is hedging a core part of risk management? If so, describe the hedging strategy used by the IMG. How effective has hedging been? What are the costs of the hedging programme?

(v)   What are the core risk tools and systems used by the IMG to manage risk?

(vi)   Do the IMG's risk management efforts incorporate any third-party risk management advisers or other similar risk management service providers?

(vii)   What other risks does the IMG face beyond risks associated with its investment strategy? Some examples could relate to key man risk, regulatory change that would impact the IMG, redemptions, etc.

(b) Operations

(i)   Identify the key operations team members and their backgrounds if not done so elsewhere.

(ii)   What are the key operational risks related to the IMG's investment strategy?

(iii)   What is the process for trade capture, confirmation, and settlement?

(iv)   Please explain how all operational processes are properly documented and that all required records are stored properly.

(v)   Are the operational processes done by staff manually or is there any process automation involved?

(vi)   When was the last major operational issue (or during the last X period of time)? Please describe. What was the profit and loss impact, if any, of the operational issue?

(vii)   Describe the escalation process if a trade error or other operational issue arises.

(c) Infrastructure

(i)   Does the IMG have a Business Continuity Plan (BCP)? If so, please describe.

(ii)   How frequently is the BCP tested? If the BCP is tested, is there an evaluation and improvements made to the BCP? Please describe.

(iii)   Has the BCP been activated for a real scenario? If so, please describe the details and the effectiveness of the BCP.

(iv)   Some prospective investors may request a copy of the IMG's BCP.

(v)   Does the IMG have an IT Policy that outlines data storage and backup policies? If so, please describe.

(vi)   Are the IMG's IT Policy, technical hardware including servers, and data back-up processes compliant with its regulator's requirements?

(vii)   Please describe the IMG's policy in the event of an IT issue such as loss of data, server issues, or cyber attack.

(viii)   Some prospective investors may request a copy of the IMG's IT Policy.

4. Compliance and Legal
   (a) Compliance
      (i) Identify the key team member(s) responsible for compliance at the IMG and their backgrounds if not done so elsewhere.
      (ii) Some prospective investors may request a copy of the IMG's Compliance Manual.
      (iii) Please describe the IMG's soft dollar policy.
      (iv) Please describe the IMG's anti-money-laundering policy.
      (v) Please describe how the IMG manages conflicts of interest.
      (vi) Please identify current conflicts of interest involving the IMG and how those conflicts of interest are being managed.
      (vii) Does the IMG use any third-party service providers to assist with its compliance function? If so, please identify.
   (b) Legal
      (i) Identify the key team member(s) responsible for legal at the IMG and their backgrounds if not done so elsewhere.
      (ii) Is the IMG currently involved in any civil or criminal litigation? Has the IMG been involved in any civil or criminal litigation the last 'X' amount of years? If so, please describe.
      (iii) Have senior members of the IMG been involved in any civil or criminal litigation? If so, please describe.
      (iv) Has the IMG, its affiliates, and/or its employees ever been part of any regulatory investigation or other similar action? If so, what was the outcome of such regulatory investigation or similar action?
      (v) Does the IMG use any third-party service providers to assist with its legal work? If so, please identify.
5. Information on the Funds that the IMG Serves
   Once information has been provided on the IMG most DDQs will ask for information on the fund(s) that the IMG serves. For convenience, reference to fund here will include a master fund and its related feeder funds ('master–feeder structure'). Generally, information on a fund will include information such as the following. The below is not an exhaustive list but should provide some guidance on what to consider when preparing a DDQ or when evaluating a DDQ. As mentioned earlier, most of this information will also be contained in the PPM.
   (a) Chart explaining the relationship between the IMG, fund, and service providers. If a master–feeder structure, then this should be depicted on the chart with annotations to indicate the legal relationship of the IMG to the fund and the legal relationship of the service providers to the fund and/or IMG. If an IMG serves more than one fund, then a chart should be created for each fund that the IMG serves.

(b) Core legal information related to the fund and subscribing to the fund. Potential investors should be provided with the fund's marketing presentation and the fund's PPM.

(c) Description of management and performance fees.

(d) Detailed description of subscription and redemption mechanics including different share classes, gate provisions, notice periods, lock-up periods, and other features should be explained clearly in order to avoid any issues in the future.

(e) Detailed description of the fund's pricing and valuation policy, which should also be outlined in the fund's PPM.

(f) Description of the method, substance, and frequency of how fund investors receive information related to their investment in the fund including performance reporting.

(g) Description and policy of the fund's use of side pockets.

(h) Name and background of the fund's directors.

   (i) Detailed background information on service providers (e.g., audit firm, custodian, law firm(s), primer broker(s), administrator, etc.) including contact information, length of appointment, and relevant details related to the service agreement between the fund and each service provider.

   (j) Some investors may ask for the fund's audited financial statements for a designated period of time. For a master–feeder arrangement, in most cases the audited financial statements of the feeder fund will be requested.

Index

Index compiled by Terry Halliday